SILENT EMBRACE

Perspectives on Birth and Adoption

Edited by Ann & Amanda Angel

D1715454

Published by Catalyst Book Press
Livermore, California

Copyright © 2010 by Ann & Amanda Angel
Cover Design: Kathy McInnis

No part of this book may be reproduced or transmitted in any form or by any means, graphic, electronic or mechanical, including photocopying, recording, taping or by any information storage or retrieval system, without permission in writing from the publisher, except in cases of brief quotations for reviews. For information, please write Catalyst Book Press at info@catalystbookpress.com.

Summary: An anthology of essays by, for, and about birth parents and the adoption triad.

ISBN 978-0-980208160
Library of Congress Control Number: 2010932212
November 2010
Printed in the United States of America

To order additional copies of the book, contact Catalyst Book Press
www.catalystbookpress.com
info@catalystbookpress.com
925-606-5992

To everyone who has been touched
by the power of adoption.

"We must overcome the notion that we must be regular...
it robs you of the chance to be extraordinary and leads you to
do the mediocre."
~ Uta Hagen

TABLE OF CONTENTS

BIRTH MOTHERS ARE WINNERS
Kimberly Horder Craig

I was curled up on the sofa in our family's living room the day my
mother sat down beside me and asked the question that would shatter
my hopes for my sophomore year of high school. Her voice was gentle
and the hand on my shoulder was calming. Her eyes searched mine for
the truth.

"Kim, have you ever had sex?"

"No." My response was immediate and reflexive. It was also a lie. I
was sixteen years old and, although my mother had always encouraged
me to come to her when I started thinking about having sex, that
was just something moms said, right? What teenage girl actually
wants to have that conversation? What mother, for that matter? My
mom, however, was an ob/gyn. She knew the signs of pregnancy and
recognized what I had not even been able to admit to myself.

"Honey, I think you're pregnant."

I felt my stomach drop, the way it does on a roller coaster. My
heart beat faster, panicked. Me, pregnant? My mother is telling me
I'm pregnant?! My head filled with all the reasons this couldn't be. *I'm
16. I'm a track star. I'm a straight A student. I never drink; I never go to
high school parties. I don't do drugs. I had sex with my boyfriend three
times. You have got to be kidding me!* As I sat on my living room sofa, I
was speechless. I had been to a doctor in my mother's ob/gyn practice
earlier that day because my stomach had been hurting. I returned
home after the appointment, but my mother had remained at work.
Suspecting that my stomach problems might be the symptom of

9

something other than a gastro-intestinal issue, she had asked that a pregnancy test be run.

One of her partners confirmed her suspicions, and now she was telling me.

I started screaming. I can't remember what I screamed because all I could hear was the rushing in my ears, like a vacuum sucking up the life I had planned. After months of ignoring physical signs, my Catholic school uniform suddenly became unbearably tight with this news.

My thoughts turned to my birth mother. She had been 16 when she had me. I was adopted at three days old. Although I was thankful for her decision to give me up, I swore I was never going to turn out like her. I was special. I had plans for an incredible life. This was not part of my blueprint.

Hysterical, unable to accept this shift in my reality, I continued to scream. "Oh my God! Oh my God! Oh my God!" I jumped off the sofa and stormed into a different room, as if I could physically move away from the truth. My mom followed me to the kitchen. The living room. The den. She tried to calm me, but I would not be calmed. Finally, still screaming with what strength I had left, I let my mom put her arm around me and bring me upstairs to my sister's bedroom in the back of the house. I was so loud that I am sure the neighbors could hear. And if they couldn't—Harry Norman could. Mr. Norman, a top Atlanta realtor, had just knocked on my parents' door. He had come to meet my mom in order to discuss photographs of our home to be placed in a local magazine's home section. My mom left me upstairs to answer the door. Today, she laughs when she describes the brief interview with Mr. Norman. She opened the door with a big smile while I continued to run around upstairs, crying and screaming. With characteristic Southern manners, she graciously informed him that "now is not a good time." Then she gently closed the door in his stunned face.

After Mr. Norman left and my mom came back upstairs, she sat beside me on my sister's bed while fearful tears rolled down my face. I could only imagine what she was thinking. Was she angry? Was she sorry she had ever adopted me? Was she ashamed? My parents were well-known in the community. My mom was the first female physician in the county and my dad was an attorney for one of the most prominent law firms in the nation. Now I was their pregnant 16-year-old daughter.

As I calmed down, my mom listed my options. My first reaction to the news that I was pregnant was to get rid of the baby. Abortion would not be out of the question; I grew up in a liberal, well-to-do family. My mother supported Planned Parenthood and was one of the few doctors in her practice who would perform a medically mandated abortion. Both Mom and Dad had discussed with me and my sister a woman's right to choose. So my answer to what I was going to do about my pregnancy was "easy." I was not going to have this baby. No one would have to know that I had even been pregnant—not my dad, not my sister, not my friends—no one. It was bad enough that my mom knew. My "easy" option, however, was made more difficult once my mom explained some details about just how pregnant I was.

"Kim, you have three choices. You can terminate this pregnancy. However, being that you are about 22 weeks along, you will need to deliver the aborted baby." She had felt and measured my belly while we were downstairs on the living room sofa. I was 5 ½ months pregnant and had not even realized it.

I closed my eyes and let go of my original plan. I was pro-choice, but the idea of delivering an aborted baby…"No," I said, knowing this was not an option for me.

"Your second option is to have and raise this baby."

Just as quickly, I knew this was not going to work either. With a child now, how would I finish high school, graduate college, become a teacher and small business owner, marry the man of my dreams and have two children by age thirty-two?!

"Your third option is to have this baby and give it up for adoption."

She told me that she and Dad would support whatever decision I made. But before she could even finish speaking, I had made up my mind. I would have this baby and give it up for adoption. I didn't know what the Lord had planned for me, my baby, and our future, but I knew He would take care of us.

Within twenty-four hours, my mom had flown my dad's mom, Nana, in from Michigan. We quickly planned for me to return with Nana to attend a small high school for pregnant teens so that I could continue my studies and graduate on time.

Together we waited anxiously for my dad to return home from a week long trip. My mom hadn't mentioned any of this to him while he was away. He needed to be home when we told him.

I watched his arrival as my mom stopped him on the front porch and told him the news. Had he made it inside, he would have thought something was terribly wrong. My Nana never just popped in for a visit. Moments later my dad came inside with tears streaming down his face and hugged me tightly. I could barely look at him.

"Kimmy, everything is going to be okay. I love you. We will get through this together."

I wasn't the first pregnant teenager my father knew. He had practiced adoption law since I was born and even wrote the very first adoption laws for the state of Georgia. Never in a million years could he have imagined one of his own baby girls unwed and pregnant at age 16.

I was so far along by the time I discovered that I was pregnant that I had the opportunity to find out the baby's sex. When my mother asked me if I wanted to find out what I was having, I didn't hesitate to say, "Yes!" If I was going to carry this baby for the next three and a half months, I wanted to know what sex it was so that I could call him or her by name. After all, this baby was mine for a little while longer.

After my mom's office had closed for the day, we drove out there so that she could perform an ultrasound on me. I was excited and nervous. Although I had not originally realized the gas in my stomach was actually a baby moving around inside me, now I was going to see this little thing!

Was it a boy or a girl? Whatever it was... what was I going to name it? I had never come up with a girl's name growing up, but while playing on the monkey bars at recess in the fourth grade, I had figured what I was going to name my first son. Did I really want to give away my name?

I remember walking through the back door that I had walked through so many times before into my mom's office. But this time I wasn't there to meet my mom for lunch or pick up a prescription. This time I would find myself on an exam table, naked from the waist down, anxiously waiting while my mother turned on the ultrasound machine and prepped the tools we would need. The gel my mom spread on my belly was cold.

Almost immediately I could see my baby on the screen. The head, eyes, and nose were perfect! I could see the feet crossed! The only thing left to see was if I was going to be having a boy or a girl. I closed my eyes as my mom searched around.

It didn't take her long.

"Kimmy?"

"Yes?"

"It's a boy!"

I cried. I'm not sure if I cried tears of joy, tears of sadness, or from thoughts of the son I was going to give away. My baby—my son—was real. This was one of those moments during this journey I will never forget.

I honestly thought that since I was over halfway through my pregnancy when I found out I was pregnant, the bond would not be able to grow as strong as it would otherwise. I would later learn I could not have been more wrong. A mother's bond is a mother's bond.

Sometimes it's funny the way life works itself out. Two weeks prior to this pivotal moment, my mom met with a couple from California who had come to Atlanta to adopt a baby. It didn't work out. Overcome with sorrow and despair, they returned home with no child. My mom understood their pain because my parents had dealt with infertility too. Their longing to become parents led them to adoption.

God had plans for this couple and for me. They would become parents. I would give them a son named Christopher and they would choose to keep his name. We set up a meeting while I was in Michigan with my Nana and attending school. My mom flew up to be with me the weekend I met this couple.

Because we had previously exchanged photos, I recognized Laura and Dave as soon as they walked off the plane. I stood there with a beautiful baby blue scrapbook and a bouquet of flowers to greet my special guests. I could see they were nervous. Who wouldn't be? But what they didn't know was that I had already decided they were the ones who would raise my son. I had learned to trust my mom's instincts. When she told me they would be wonderful parents, I trusted her. I spoke with Laura and Dave on several occasions and exchanged photos before our meeting. We talked about our hobbies, favorite foods, lifelong dreams, interests and values. While we had very little in common other than our faith, I could not have hand-picked more suitable parents for my son. After our weekend together, my gut feelings were confirmed.

This month, June 2009, marks the 15th anniversary of Christopher's adoption.

I remember so clearly when Christopher was born. My labor could not have been more perfect. He was so tiny, six pounds and seven ounces. He was so beautiful; I held him, memorizing his face, gently tracing the smooth silk of his skin with the pad of my finger. With my mom and my sister by my side, I held him tightly. I couldn't stop staring at him. Nothing else around me mattered. This was my son.

I was his mother for now. I kept Christopher in the room with me the entire time I was in the hospital. I changed his diapers and fed him all of his bottles. He was not leaving my sight until it was time.

It was important for me to baptize my son before I said good-bye. Reverend Lori came out to the hospital to perform the ceremony. My mom, sister, dad and brother were all there along with Laura and Dave, Christopher's adoptive parents. At the beginning of the Baptism,

I clearly remember that I handed Christopher to Laura to hold. It's been 15 years and it is still painful to remember. I was sitting up in the hospital bed. Laura and Dave were to my right. I asked Laura if she wanted to hold him, and she said, "Yes."

I gave him to her.

I began to weep silently and, when I handed Christopher to her, he started to cry. I remember thinking, *It's because I'm his mother.*

After the baptism, Laura and Dave left to stay with family friends until the next day—the day when I would say good-bye and they would become his parents.

I held Christopher all night long. The nurses would come in urging me to put him down so I could sleep. There would be plenty of time to sleep later. Putting him down was unthinkable. I stared at him while he slept. I stared at him while he ate. I stared at him staring right back at me.

He knew who I was. He knew that I loved him more than anything else in the world.

Morning came quickly. I had been dreading this day for months. I had my mom and my sister at my side with me in my final moments with my son. My dad remained at home. He had witnessed a birth mother's good-bye many times. He could not watch his daughter say good-bye to his grandson. It was too painful.

Before I even began getting ready for the day, Dr. Campbell, my physician, came in at my mom's request to make sure that I wanted to give Christopher up for adoption. She asked if this was my decision and if I felt comfortable with it.

Grateful that she had taken this time for me, I assured her that this was what I wanted to do. I knew I was doing what was best for me and my baby.

I remember taking a shower and my mom blow drying my hair. We had picked out my going home outfit weeks before. It wasn't a maternity outfit, but it was a beautiful, comfortable dark red shorts and shirt set. I had plans to wear it again. After I was ready, we dressed Christopher in his going home outfit.

I had picked it out just for him. I tucked his tiny hands and feet into the baby blue and white baseball sleep n' play, then placed the matching hat on his head. He looked handsome. It pleased me to think they would think he was handsome too. We took pictures of Christopher with us. My mom took a Polaroid of me and Christopher so we could leave it with him.

It is incredibly painful, even now, to remember my good-bye. Holding him that last time—knowing it was the last time—felt as if someone had ripped out all my insides and I had nothing left. I knew this pain would linger, not just disappear.

I was about to lose my first child.

I remember walking out of the hospital room so composed. I chose not to look back. The walk down the hallway seemed like eternity.

I remember getting to the car.

My sister and mom helped me put my bags in the car. My mom said, "All right, girls, I have to drive home. We'll cry when we get there."

And so we did.

In the darkness that followed Christopher's birth, I believed that this was all a part of a larger plan the Lord had for me. This faith is what got me through the difficult times that followed. There were numerous nights that I cried myself to sleep.

Though Christopher was out of sight, the reminders of his birth were still with me. For most women, the experience of having their baby's milk come in provides tangible, physical validation of their role as mother. For me, it was painful. I remember stretching an ace bandage around my breasts for days to stop milk from producing. But this takes time. When I took showers, the hot water would stimulate milk production, and I would stand under the stream watching milk flow freely down my chest, down my legs and into the drain.

It was a physical reminder that couldn't be denied. I had given birth to a son who would never need my nourishment.

For the first few days following Christopher's birth, I carried around a box with his things. I had his first pacifier, first blanket, hospital bracelets and first pictures. They were mine, and no one was going to take them away from me. In time, my baby box went from the top of the fireplace in my bedroom, to my bookshelf, to the bottom of my bookshelf, and finally to my closet where it remained for many years.

I started running three days after his birth and was back to my pre-pregnancy weight within two weeks. Running was my medicine. When I returned to my Catholic high school, I had a cross-country season ahead of me and less than two months to prepare. I planned to make sure I had my best season yet. Fellow classmates could whisper all they wanted, but I worked to be skinny and fast. There would be no physical clues from the past to give people more reason to talk.

I survived high school. The journey of Christopher's adoption brought me a strength that could not have been granted me otherwise. In fact, I excelled. I received numerous athletic and academic awards during my high school career. One of my greatest accomplishments was being chosen as one of two graduates in my class to be an Olympic Torch Escort Runner in the 1996 Atlanta Olympic Games. I had won. *I was a winner.*

I went on to graduate college with a Bachelor's Degree in Business and marry the man of my dreams. My husband Shawn and I became pregnant with our first son shortly after we married and I had begun teaching. I can't remember ever being more excited! I was pregnant with my baby. A baby that would be mine forever. A son that I was going to raise. I would see his first step. I would see his first little league game. I would someday watch his graduations and his walk down the aisle with his new bride.

The entire family waited with anticipation for the arrival of our little man, Shawn-Michael, Jr. He would be the first grandbaby on either side of the family. Ironically, he was born in June, the same month as Christopher. I would return to the very hospital I had been to nine years before. However, this time would be a celebration.

On the day he was born, the room was packed. I had my sister and mother-in-law on my right side with my father-in-law behind them with the video camera. Shawn was to my left with my father behind him to catch him if he fell. My mom stood at the foot of the delivery table. She would be the first to welcome my son into the world.

I remember looking at my mom as she guided me through. She never stopped smiling at me. After less than fifteen minutes of pushing, my son was born. My mom stood up and laid him on my tummy, but not before she kissed her new grandson on the forehead. He was beautiful, perfect and mine! Shawn's pulse felt as though it would jump out of his body. My dad stood speechless. My father-in-law cheered. My sister laughed and wept. My mother-in-law grinned from ear to ear. And I cried the most joyful tears. I felt fulfilled. Complete. Nothing could take this moment away from me.

I was so excited to nurse. In fact, I hurried everyone out of the room. As I gazed at this baby peacefully nursing at my breast, I could not help but think of another baby that I had held in this hospital and the woman who was now his mother. It felt *right* that Laura had experienced a similar beautiful moment with Christopher, *her* son, nine years before, and now the right time had come for me to have this shimmering, glittering moment with *my* son.

This transfer of the role of mother from one woman to another and the love that two women feel for a child is the magic and mystery of adoption.

Motherhood has been such a blessing. I am grateful that such an emotionally painful experience I had as a teenager was able to be transformed into an opportunity for another woman to become a mother. I am grateful that Christopher has loving, supportive parents who are able to provide the stable family that he deserves. And I am grateful that I am able to experience motherhood for the first time with joy and hope rather than fear and anxiety. Adoption made winners of all of us, but I think especially me, the birth mother.

18

SURRENDERING HOLLY
Patti Cleary

Jinni, my gorgeous and ebullient thirty-something neighbor, stops by the other day with her newborn, Cooper. As we marvel about what a good baby he is, she starts to raise a breastfeeding issue. She breaks off mid sentence to ask, "Did *you* nurse?"

I realize that at some point I must have divulged some tidbit about my own long ago birthing experience. The pause grows longer, and Jinni's voice falters as she attempts to fill the awkward silence.

"Uh...do you have children?"

Ouch. There it is—the question that has plagued me so many times. What do I say that won't require lengthy discourse or introduce a downer into this pleasant exchange? That won't diminish a life experience of paramount proportions? And why after so many years have I not come up with a more effective response than what I stammer through now?

"It's...uh....sort of a long story."

Thorny topic dismissed, we return to the safer ground of admiring little Cooper.

Do I have children? No, I do not. Did I give birth to a daughter, surrender her for adoption, and then for many decades struggle mightily with the impact of this decision? Oh, verily yes. And did I heed the advice to forget about it and move on with my life? Ha! What jokesters were those well-intentioned advisers.

Further complicating the experience of loss were my feelings for Mike, my baby's young father. He was everything desired by a naïve young woman who had not yet matured into her future strong, independent self. He was cute, smart, aloof, dismissive, and cruel. Be still my hungry, seventeen-year-old heart.

Our senior year in high school found us skipping class to conduct amorous forays at Mike's house while his parents were at work. We never once discussed or used birth control. Why not? Because it was awkward for minors to purchase forbidden items seemingly reserved for grownups. No store displays graced counters in 1966. You had to ask the pharmacist who might glare, throw you out of the store, or phone your parents. A boy might carry a crumpled, sealed condom in his wallet as a status symbol; a girl would never do such a thing. Also discouraging birth control use was the issue of premeditation.

For me to admit to myself or to Mike that we were engaging in sexual activity was to brand myself outwardly with labels that the inward self tried to dodge—bad girl, tramp, slut. We were playing at having sex, at being adults, and it was fun but surely not a serious exchange of caring. Still, I did care. Very much.

My best friend Carolyn, already a mom, had been forced to leave school the year before. I relied on her for guidance, from where to go to get diagnosed to how to break the news to Mike and my parents. I was more fortunate, because I didn't become pregnant until spring of senior year. I was seventeen, though I would turn eighteen just before my baby was born. My petite frame didn't begin to show until my seventh month, and I attended senior prom looking radiant and slightly voluptuous, after which I was able to graduate.

I assumed that, like Carolyn, I would marry and grow up fast as I struggled to cope with scary new responsibilities. Our cohorts seemed to navigate fairly well through this well-established trajectory of bad news, rapid-fire scandal, quickie wedding, and novice parenthood. Others, shrouded in secrecy, disappeared for a time, explaining their absence with tales of caring for an ailing grandparent or visiting a distant cousin.

When I told Mike the news, I expected him to be upset and believed that once he adjusted (quickly, of course), we could begin to plan our life together as a young family. I would not be able to go to college as planned but he could attend part time and work. Sacrifice? Surely, but that was the consequence of "getting in trouble." Except that he didn't see it that way. Not at all.

"I'm sorry," he said. "I can't marry you. I wish I could, but the truth is I don't want to. I refuse to ruin my life over this."

I was devastated to hear these words but told myself that he just needed more time. I was certain he would experience a change of heart, an illusion I clung to for months of being pregnant that gave way to years of struggling to cope with the aftermath. As long as two decades later, a spark of that hope survived.

Throughout girlhood, I had been socialized to anticipate pregnancy as an extraordinary interlude of joyous expectation. Instead, my pregnancy was a time of regret and shame. On one occasion, when my parents were renewing their life insurance policy, their agent stopped by to collect a payment. I was asked to hide in the basement so as not to risk the levy of a higher premium. Unfortunately, he was chatty and would stay for an hour or longer.

Although the insurance agent never discovered that I was pregnant, nearly everyone else did. I could offer no cover up story or hastily arranged nuptials to spare me the disgrace of being pregnant with no plans to make it right in the eyes of the community.

My hope that Mike would reconsider lived on, however, so I tried to make the best of my situation while I waited him out. While he and my college-bound classmates matriculated, I moved in with a single working mom and her four children. I earned a little money by caring for the kids. My parents and Mike's had not resolved how to deal with expenses, leaving me with no money for maternity clothes or prenatal care and no idea where my baby would be born. I borrowed a few items of maternity garb from Carolyn. I loved the kids I cared for, but unable to go to school, I found it hard to endure phone calls from Mike ranting about annoying college bureaucracy. One day I took the kids for a walk in their quiet neighborhood. Sporting a hot pink maternity top over purple pants and self-conscious about my new tendency to waddle, I felt like a fat-assed Easter Bunny. I was horrified to pass a snobby rich girl, a classmate who had tried to steal Mike away from me. As excruciating waves of shame washed over me, I prayed she didn't recognize me. She didn't acknowledge me, but that was no guarantee that she wouldn't have a juicy anecdote to pass along.

My thoughts focused on the big decision that lay ahead should Mike not change his mind. My mother let me know that she would support any choice I made.

My father challenged the viability of surrender. "No one will ever love that baby the way that you will," he advised. Ironic, this perspective from the alcoholic who often referred to himself as "Bad Dad," a moniker earned with verbally and physically abusive behaviors. His habit of coming home drunk and mean was one of the primary reasons I felt I must surrender my child.

A pregnant schoolmate who planned to marry insisted that I could not abandon my child while another, already married because of an unplanned pregnancy, told me she regretted her choice. Both, however, had husbands, and I contemplated having none. I was afraid that I could not manage the responsibility. I was afraid that I would not manage the loss.

I anticipated a difficult labor, my punishment for exhibiting behavior unbecoming a young woman of the 1960s. Instead, I delivered a month early, needing to spend just a few days at the unwed mothers' home. Those who'd been there for months gave me, with affection, a hard time. I arrived late at night, after a day of strange physical sensations. The doctor on duty pronounced false labor. I was nearly sent home, but because it was an hour's drive, they decided to keep me overnight. They isolated me on a deserted wing to minimize contact with other residents, consistent with those Secret Shame principles that informed the era's out-of-wedlock pregnancy experience. Installed in my isolated room, I continued to feel pressure but nothing I could define as labor pains. Someone came by to check on me, and suddenly I was being prepped for delivery. If a difficult labor was to be my punishment, I clearly escaped it. In the early hours of New Year's Eve day, I experienced maybe four hard pushes and out she came. Tiny but not preemie, they told me.

As she left my body, I sensed that something was wrong. I was told that the umbilical cord was wound tightly around her neck. Woozy from anesthesia, I was aware of tubes thrust into my nose and this urgent command, "Breathe for your baby!" In a split second, I considered that since I wasn't going to be able to do much for this child, I could at least suck in some seriously lung-filling air. I inhaled so deeply, each breath seemed to contract the delivery room walls. Soon I was reassured—all was fine. Whew. An hour and ten minutes after they left me at the facility, my parents returned home to a ringing telephone and were duly informed that my daughter had been born.

I continued to halfway believe in a change of heart from Mike even after his displays of juvenile cruelty the evening of our daughter's birth. At a New Year's Eve party with many of our friends, one reported that at midnight, Mike raised his glass to fatherhood with cavalier sarcasm. The next day he accompanied my parents to the unwed mothers' home, where he spent a few minutes beholding his newborn daughter through the nursery window. During the ride home, he said to my parents, "Well, wasn't much of a baby, was it?" Was this his evaluation of her small stature, at four pounds thirteen ounces? Or his attempt to mask feelings of regret? I'm still astonished that my father didn't murder him then and there, but apparently the presence of my little sister restrained him. What a creep. A creep I loved, no doubt. Darker still, this reality: I felt I deserved such poor treatment.

A day later came the visit from my dowdy social worker, the one I'd met with several times during my pregnancy. She'd met with Mike, too. I'd advised him to follow my plan to impress her with my intelligence so that our baby would be placed with a family that would expect to raise a smart child who should be sent to college. "Use big words—lots of syllables!" I urged Mike. Here she was, in my room at the unwed mothers' home, toting a battered briefcase. She extracted a series of documents that I was to sign to officially relinquish my baby. She explained each document and passed it to me.

As I started to sign, she said, "Wait. Look at me." Her usual kind manner replaced with unforgiving sternness and a penetrating glare, she repeated, "I want you to look at me now."

I did as she commanded.

"I want you to tell me something. How does it feel to sign away your own flesh and blood?"

I was not prepared for this switcheroo. What happened to the gentle assurances that life would go on and I could feel that I had done the selfless thing by surrendering my baby? I felt required to show that I felt not just contrite but also ashamed. No problem there. Still, awash in post-delivery hormonal surges, I would spend years trying to sort out the storm of emotions attached to this moment. I managed to shed a few tears so that she would leave me alone, which she did, but not until proclaiming, "Stay away from him. If you don't, you'll be back here in a year."

I had the option of holding my baby one time only, for thirty minutes. One of the unwed mothers' home residents who was expecting twins assured all of us that she would be granted thirty minutes with each of her babies, an opportunity she longed for. Another had that same day held her new baby boy but was struggling to cope with what would come next when her parents, who were adopting him, would represent him to the world as her brother.

Though I yearned to hold my daughter, I feared that physical touch would make separating from her even more unbearable. I elected not to hold her and claimed that I wouldn't see her either. But when my parents headed for the nursery window, something made me rise and follow them, despite my plan to avoid contact. And there she was—tiny, beautiful. A very pregnant resident earning her keep at the home by

24

working as a nurse held up my baby girl and announced that though she was tiny, she still sported a wee pot belly. My parents and I laughed, delighted to behold her, but our joy was tempered by the painful reality that in another day, we would not see her again.

I left the home for unwed mothers, glad to return to "normal" life yet not fully aware of how difficult it would be. The first glimpse emerged as I unpacked my suitcase. My mother had forbidden me to tell my ten-year-old brother of my pregnancy. Her uniquely suppressive logic? Maybe he doesn't know, so don't upset him. But my suspicion that he did know was now confirmed as he tiptoed into my room whispering, "Where is the baby?"

Fresh from the numbing shock of leaving my daughter, I now must explain to my kid brother that I had given her away. Welcome home.

I struggled to regain my footing in the world, starting college mid-year at our local university, a semester after my former classmates had begun their studies. When I encountered them on campus, their initial reaction was unsettling. Examples included, "Hey, I didn't see you last semester—where were you?" Or, "How are you and Mike and the baby doing?"

Each time I had to try to satisfy the questioner while discouraging further discourse. To this day, some questions still throw me, especially "Do you have children?" because "Kinda," or "Not really" don't feel like appropriate responses.

However challenging I found this transition, the times ahead would prove far more difficult. Initially, I had to contend with the physical ache in arms that longed to hold my baby. Years later, a nurse friend explained that this sensation occurs frequently among mothers coping with stillbirth.

I worked my way through decades of internal struggle, evolving from shame and guilt through guilt-driven behaviors and eventually to some degree of resolution and peace. I became a teacher and, though I taught junior high students, I would scan the playground when it was filled with younger kids, hoping to catch sight of someone who looked like me, who looked like she might look.

After years of dreading New Year's Eve, awash in feelings of loss, regret, and longing, I began to do some research. I contacted someone associated with Concerned United Birthparents (CUB) who advised me to create some health information that should be passed on and to use this as leverage to gain access to information. I do understand this need to know/right to know perspective but much of my own experience was tainted with intense feelings of shame and guilt. Having internalized this sinfulness, I felt that I had no right to know anything, really. Ultimately I wasn't ready to attend a CUB meeting. Although I sensed empathy, participating felt too painful to even contemplate.

A few years later, the longing tugged at me again. I mustered the courage to phone the agency that had facilitated my surrender. Perhaps it was the sternness of the woman I'd dealt with years before and the degree to which I had internalized "bad girl" judgments, but I didn't expect to be treated well. Thus it was a surprise to be greeted warmly and invited to meet with their representative. During this meeting, I received concrete information about my birth daughter, more than I thought I would, though it was classified as "non-identifying." I was also encouraged to join a birth mothers' group. I was nervous when I attended the first session with these women with whom I expected to identify. After several sessions, however, I decided that if several of them had been my birth mother, I might not have wanted to know. Still, I learned much from this group about what NOT to do should I ever have the chance to reunite.

At one meeting, the group hosted an adoptive mother. She bravely faced a small audience that seemed to have no gratitude for the role she played in her adopted child's life. Throughout the exchange that took place that night, I was surprised to discover that I identified more with the woman who had adopted than with the group of women who had surrendered. The tone from the birth mothers was spiked with resentment, something in hindsight I would characterize as misdirected pain and anger. At the time, I thought it unkind and rude.

One demanded, "Do you ever think of your child's mother? Of US?"

The adoptive mother politely responded, "Well, I feel that I AM my child's mother."

In another session, a woman who had just met her surrendered son for the first time described this life-changing experience. She was thrilled and effusive, and I was happy for her…and also jealous. She told us of her delight in learning that both she and her son liked Italian food, as if this signaled some significant genetic connection.

How naïve!

"I told him about my suicide attempt," she confided.

Dumb shit, I thought.

Another woman struck me as a weepy whiner. Her daughter had agreed to meet with her but then wanted no further contact.

I recognized the tragedy of having to experience the loss all over again, but when this woman recounted how she showed up, uninvited, at her birth daughter's wedding, she seemed more like a misguided stalker than a victim of difficult circumstances.

The most tragic figure was a young woman, pregnant at age 14, whose parents refused to let her marry the boy she loved and insisted that she surrender their baby. She later married the young man and then discovered they were no longer able to bear children. They were determined to find their child. I hope they succeeded.

I arranged to meet with the adoption specialist who facilitated this birth mothers' group. While reviewing the agency files, she told me of my birth daughter's good performance in grade school. My heart swelled with joy and something else—pride. But I promptly reminded myself that I was NOT ENTITLED to take "credit" for any gains she had made in life.

Soon after this session, I left the birth mothers' group, which had encouraged me to hope for a reunion but not to count on one happening. I also learned what not to do if a reunion did materialize:

don't move in too fast, don't show up at the second meeting with my entire extended family, and don't feel compelled to unload intense and personal information too soon. Though we birth mothers might be harboring intense unmet needs, unloading these on our birth children would be selfish and could scare them away.

The adoption specialist, a warm, well-spoken woman, helped me grapple with some of the loss issues. She said that adoptees who are content with their life are less likely to search. Seekers tend to search during times of personal transition such as marriage, childbirth, or the death of their adoptive parents. She told me some adoptees asked for information and wanted nothing further while others longed for a reunion meeting that was denied. She characterized the experience of the adoptee as one of being taken in as compared to that of the birth parent as one of loss and letting go. I tried to grasp all of this wisdom. She recommended that I write a letter to my daughter, include photos, and address questions that typically arose. What are you like? Whom do I look like? Did you marry my birth father? Was your life ruined by this experience? Do you ever think of me? Why did you surrender me? I put this assignment off for a few weeks, needing time to absorb the new information about my daughter and the experience of the birth mothers' group.

I worked on the letter for most of a gray, cold day. I told my daughter that I had never forgotten her, would very much like to know about her, and would welcome her into my life if that made sense for her. This letter had to be approved by the adoption specialist before it could be placed on file where it would remain until such time as my daughter might reach out to the agency that had arranged the adoption.

Soon after this, I reached a decision about whether I'd continue to search. I hoped my daughter would follow the trail I'd left, but I knew there was no guarantee that she would. I had also learned that some will not search until their adoptive parents die because they feel guilty about needing to seek out their birth parents. And it seems that some adoptive parents do contend with feelings of betrayal.

I resolved not to impose myself by searching and to let my daughter make the choice to reach out, even if it meant I might never meet her. It seemed to me that I didn't have the right to look for her, no matter how much I might long to know her and how much I needed to learn if I had done the right thing in surrendering her. The answers to these yearnings had haunted me for years—was she okay? Was she healthy? Was she even alive? Did she wear braces? Did she hate vegetables? Was she struggling to be happy? I had ached to know the answers to these and a zillion other questions but had also felt not entitled to know them.

Having taken steps to welcome her to my life, I felt some degree of release from the pain of relinquishing her. Placing this letter in the hands of the agency, I went on with my life, feeling more at peace, and I no longer dreaded New Year's Eve. Although I still harbored expectations to bear one or more children, the opportunity never materialized and thus the daughter I'd left behind represented my one shot at progeny.

One day a few months after I'd placed the letter, I was running an errand when someone caught my eye.

"Mr. H_____, is that you?" It was Mike's father, whom I hadn't seen in twenty years.

I was surprised at the warmth with which he greeted me. In the past, he'd been angry and unforgiving. We launched a new connection that day, supported by phone calls, visits, and holiday cards.

At some point he said, "Look, I didn't want you to marry Mike because I thought you'd ruin his life. But he's done that all on his own without you. And you seem to have done quite well for yourself."

It was hard not to find this turnaround gratifying. I eventually told him I'd left a trail I hoped my daughter would follow, and he was compassionate and encouraging.

A few years later, I received a phone message from the adoption agency, asking me to call them. I phoned back right away but it was

Friday evening, and the offices were closed. Could this be the call I had long hoped for? Was it just an administrative item needing my attention? Or could this be bad news coming my way? The anticipation of the next several days would prove to be intense.

Strangely enough, the next day Mike's father phoned to tell me that Mike would soon return from his adopted Swedish homeland for a visit and wanted to see me. If I agreed, it would be the first time I'd seen him in twenty years. I mentioned nothing to his father about the call from the agency.

On Monday, I arose earlier than usual, eager to be the first to call after the agency opened. Alas, a blizzard had moved in overnight, and no one answered as I continued to dial their number again and again. I chided myself that, after waiting twenty years, surely I could wait another twenty-four hours. A very long day and night followed. The next morning, I braved icy roads to drive straight to the agency and asked to see the adoption specialist. Nearly sick with anxiety, the ten minutes I was made to wait felt like hours. Finally, the small elevator opened into the lobby and out stepped the specialist.

"Hello! How are you? Come on up," she greeted me.

As I followed her into the elevator for the short trip to her office, I said, "I don't know why I'm here."

"I know," she said. "Just have a seat." Deposited in her office, I was left alone with no hints.

After an eternal minute or two, she returned, sat down, and said, "I have a letter and photos for you from your birth daughter. Would you like to see them?"

I was stunned. Thrilled. Scared. Frozen. I stammered, "Uh….of... course."

She handed me a small but thick envelope and left me to examine its contents, which I did with a hunger so intense that it frightened me.

With hands shaking, I removed a letter and two photographs. As my eyes devoured these treasures, my head reeled, and my heart fought to absorb the enormity of this windfall.

Over the next few weeks, I read that letter more than one hundred times. I soaked up every nuance, from the curve of the letters formed by someone who was no longer a ghost defined only by my speculation to the questions that I would struggle to answer not just for me but now for her as well. The letter gave me a few concrete facts as well as the delicious knowledge that her name was Holly. At last, I may know her name! And this revelation: she was attending the same university I had graduated from and thus residing quite close to me. But her letter also delivered the reality check that, though she had issued from my body, though I now could think of her by name, Holly was still a stranger to me. I longed to change that reality and now let myself hope, just a little, that I might soon have the opportunity to do so.

I set aside a day to reply to my birth daughter's letter. I weighed every syllable with great care, drawing on lessons learned from my participation in the birth mother's group. I did my best to answer some of her questions and encouraged her to consider meeting with me but was quick to assure that I did not mean to pressure her—only if and when she might be ready would we meet.

While I awaited a response, synchronicity raged and I heard from Mike. I agreed to meet him the following day, knowing I'd get no sleep that night. I considered not telling him that I'd heard from our daughter but realized it might be another twenty years before I'd hear from him again. I thought it unfair that I had longed for decades for some sort of contact while he, who had shown no interest, had just happened to return to the states when Holly was poised to reenter my life.

Mike and I had agreed to meet in the park outside my office. What would he be like now? Would the chemistry between us have survived the decades? And would he see how much I had changed from the insecure teenager who felt fortunate that he liked me and shared his belief that he had been "dating down" to the self-assured career woman I'd become?

I spotted him on a park bench. His hair had thinned considerably and his face had become more angular. His boyish cuteness was no more. Trying not to outpace him, I guided him several blocks to my parked car, mostly in awkward silence broken only by his raspy demand, "Do you always walk like this?" Here was a reminder of the disdain I recalled so well.

"I like to walk fast," I said. No apologies, not this time.

We had dinner together and conversation flowed but soon found its way back to tension and guardedness. I mentioned our birth daughter but said nothing about recent revelations.

He did not react. Driving him home to his father's, our talk eased once more. He joked that his dad would like to see us together and reunited with our child.

I did not mention that, after all these years, I still harbored a flicker of the same hope. I parked in the driveway, took out the envelope, and removed the photograph. I quickly explained that I'd heard from Holly the week before and now anticipated meeting her.

He grabbed the photo, looked at it for two seconds, placed it face down on the dash, and announced, "I'm disappointed. She looks like you. I always thought she'd look like me."

Beholding his balding pate, the gaunt visage with its angular bones, I thought, "Thank gawd she doesn't look like you." But in the years ahead, I would recognize that she does resemble each of us and bears some of our traits as well.

Mike soon returned to Sweden, and I never saw him again. In the weeks that followed, I focused on Holly. I had hoped that she would reply quickly to my letter and agree to meet, but though she did correspond with me over the next couple months, she never directly addressed my gentle requests to see her. It was May and she would soon finish her junior year and be gone for the summer.

I wrote and asked outright to see her. "Life is short," I said. "Can we please arrange to meet?" I suggested we spend an hour or two getting to know a bit more about each other. My agency contact would provide a neutral location.

I was thrilled when Holly agreed to see me on the date I proposed.

The day before we met, I let go of the myriad worries about what to wear, how to present myself, what to say first, and other forms of anxiety about making it a perfect meeting. In the end, I just lived my way through it. I'd already absorbed the reality of my first response to her photo—she is a stranger to me. My expectations in check and my nerves electrified, I arrived before she did and waited for her in a small conference room. Our agency contact brought her in, introduced and then left us. It soon became obvious that we were both chatty. As we talked, tentatively at first and then with greater ease, I drank in what I could—her face, her eyes, her demeanor.

At one point she chuckled and the hair stood up on my neck as I recognized one of my laughs, something she surely did not learn but had inherited from me. We had each brought photos to share but it was well past an hour before we reached for them. Once we did, another hour quickly flew by. And then another. I might have kept at it all day, but when I learned that her boyfriend had brought her and had been waiting all this time in his car, I suggested we stop. I could do this because I sensed that things had gone so well that I would be able to see her again. I also felt inclined to leave on a good note and to take some time to digest all the emotions that had assailed me during this meeting.

I walked her to the car and said good-bye. She made a little "awwww" sound of regret, so I bravely asked, "May I hug you?" She nodded, and as we embraced in a parking lot, I felt the angels sing, marking the sweetest moment of my life.

I raced home to phone my mother and give her a full report. I then floated into work, arriving much later than planned after this tumultuous meeting. I told my boss, who was also my friend, every detail of this romantic reunion. I recall that she tried to share my glow but, out of concern for me, mostly cautioned me not to expect too much. I knew that the heights of this experience increased the likelihood of a fall, but I didn't care. I relished the joy that washed over me. I let no one rain even a single drop on my parade. The rains would indeed descend in stormy squalls—but not today, this my day to rejoice.

Holly had also harbored romantic notions, confessing that she had phoned and hung up a couple times and had considered looking up my address and showing up on my doorstep with flowers.

When we met again a month or two later at a casual neighborhood restaurant, I brought my mother. I cherish a photo of the three of us around the patio table. Holly liked my mother, whose natural use of humor and easygoing ways made the gathering comfortable and enjoyable.

Over the next two years, I would gradually introduce Holly to other family members. Even "Bad Dad" got his moment but only after stern warnings from me not to make a big fuss, to treat Holly as a family friend. He and everyone else managed to strike the right tone.

Soon after, we met Holly's boyfriend and learned that she was pregnant and they planned to marry. Though I was not able to attend her wedding, because she did not want her parents to know we had met, I did take her shopping for her bridal veil and was thrilled when she agreed to let me purchase it. I felt gratified that in some sense I was participating in a major life event. Similarly, I jumped at the chance to take her for a prenatal care visit. We heard her baby's heartbeat together for the first time—a treasured moment. Over the next few years, we were in touch fairly regularly, and it was a thrill to spend time with my birth grandson, Ryan.

Meanwhile, my professional life was in a spin as I was offered for the third time a distant opportunity on the West Coast. Ready for a job change, I began to consider this major move. Would my daughter feel that I was again abandoning her? Did she really need me or did she just enjoy our occasional visits and phone calls? In early 1990, I took the plunge and moved 2,500 miles away.

I spent the next year settling in to a new life. The change was good, the climate was welcoming, and the opportunities for new experiences and friendships were gratifying. Holly and I spent a lot of time on the phone and we wrote letters, too. She often asked my advice and as much as I loved being perceived as the Answer Woman, she would sometimes ask me things that I had no knowledge of, such as "Should I make my own baby food?"

I would call baby food companies and request ingredient lists and send them on to her, something I could do, but what I wanted to say was, "You must know I have no experience here and that the reason I don't is uncomfortable."

It seemed that Holly was auditioning for Super Mom. I read somewhere that adoptees often aspire to be the perfect parent as a result of their having been surrendered, their method of doing better than what was done to them. The same source suggested that an opposite parenting style sometimes applied.

When Ryan reached the age of three, something shifted. Holly took a job at a local restaurant chain and, in our frequent phone conversations, began to convey a different picture of the new nuclear family. She was clearly not too thrilled with her husband. Of greater concern, she mentioned that she'd been working the late shift, staying after to hang out with coworkers. At some point, she confessed that she was doing cocaine and sleeping until noon. Where was Super Mom now?

I'd always struggled with who I was supposed to be with Holly. I knew I could never expect to be her mother. I didn't feel "friend" was the right designation either but it was as close as I could get. Now that I saw her making choices that spelled danger, I was doubly conflicted. I didn't want to be complicit but I also didn't want her to stop calling me.

The crisis came when she told me that she was pregnant again, but with another man's child. A man who was married with children and potentially abusive, too. She'd told her husband and expressed some incredulity that he was so angry about it.

I struggled to come to grips with this news and to determine how best to react to it.

I suggested she might consider surrendering the baby though I couldn't characterize this as an easy solution. I also recommended terminating the pregnancy and learned that we held dissimilar positions on this issue.

"That would be like taking a gun and shooting Ryan in the head," she claimed. A few weeks later, she let me know that when she told her "real" mother the news, she had immediately suggested terminating the pregnancy. This made Holly very angry. She said, "It's because of her that I have these values and as soon as the chips are down, she's no longer true to them?"

It seemed that everyone Holly consulted advocated a similar path except for a 19-year old friend who thought it was "cool" that Holly was pregnant, encouraged her to keep the baby, and offered to babysit.

I guess this is what she wanted to hear and so this is the advice she followed.

And then Holly stopped writing and calling. When I phoned her, she did not respond. After many weeks of no contact, I received a call from her husband. He said she'd given birth to a daughter, Danielle, and he knew that she would want me to know.

When I told him I hadn't heard from her in months, he was shocked and asked why. I told him the truth—I had no real understanding of why she had ceased to communicate with me.

Nearly a year later, as she was preparing to divorce, she did write to ask me about a financial matter. Then I got another letter in which she said she was really angry with me.

I wrote back and said I was sorry that she had bad feelings that I may have caused and that I wished we could have had a relationship that worked better.

She wrote back—the nastiest letter I've ever received—and unloaded on me. She clearly took my missive as a dismissal and rejection, yet I meant only to acknowledge her feelings, to express regret but also to sidestep any attempts to use me as a punching bag.

She wrote: "I used to feel sorry for poor Patti, pregnant and alone at 17. No more. You took the easy way out."

I was devastated but also felt that I was at last witnessing her true feelings as she was finally getting in touch with them.

Years passed during which Holly would occasionally send my mother a holiday card, enclosing photos of her children, which my mother would immediately forward to me. I learned that Holly had moved to Florida, finished college, and become an elementary school teacher. I was back to longing, a familiar enough feeling. After eleven years on the West Coast, I resettled in Delaware. One of the letters Holly sent to my mother offered an email address. I thought about emailing her but was fearful of being rejected and so held back. But the door was about to reopen in any case.

My mother received a letter from Mike, still living in Sweden. Unable to reach me, he'd sent a letter for Holly summarizing research he'd done on his ancestors in case she might be interested. He mentioned several extant journal articles he'd written, but he asked nothing whatsoever about her. My mother and I agreed that she would forward this letter to Holly, and because this was Holly's first ever contact with her birth father, she found it seriously wanting and became enraged.

She wrote to ask my mother if I would be willing to speak to her about it. And so we began to communicate, after a seven-year hiatus, bonding over what a jerk he was. "Is he trying to make me feel stupid?" she demanded. "Am I supposed to know what 'extant' means?"

Holly and I kept in touch via email for the next few years. I then had a chance to take a business trip close to her home. I asked if I could visit, giving her license to say no. When she agreed, I asked if I could meet her "real" parents.

No way, she said. She'd already hurt them enough.

I had to respect this though I dearly wanted to know them and to thank them. Would I be able to see Ryan, now 18 years old, whom I'd not seen since he was 3? And 13 year old Danielle, whom I'd seen only in photos? No guarantees. I could tell it would depend on how things went between Holly and me.

My business meeting concluded, I made the two hour drive to her coastal town, checked into my hotel, and started to sweat. As much as I had persuaded myself to believe that there was not much at stake, I was afraid to see Holly. I was to phone her but I stalled, trying to gain my bearings so that I could sound normal when I did call. I got through and we arranged to meet at a restaurant in a couple hours. I arrived early and put us on the reservation list. I waited outside on a bench, surrounded by a multitude also waiting to be seated. Would I recognize her instantly after so many years, or would it take a few seconds—or longer? Should I hug her? Probably not. I can't recall the prelude to any first date more nerve wracking than this rendezvous. I waited a good fifteen minutes.

Finally, she appeared. At first glance, a tidal wave of emotion struck, translated as: I LOVE LOVE LOVE you. Parents tell me that they experience this sensation all the time when beholding their offspring, but it was new to me. I kept my cool, of course, and smiled hello.

She was reserved, returning a small, controlled smile only.

Our dining experience started off somewhat awkwardly but our chattiness came to the rescue, and soon we were engaged in conversation that flowed fairly well. She invited me to her home the following day, when I got to see my grandchildren and spend some time with them. I also got to meet someone she had been dating, bringing to life some of the tales she'd recounted about struggling to find happiness in a relationship.

I could have flown home on Monday but it was my birthday and I thought flying, not my favorite pastime, was a lousy way to celebrate. I hadn't mentioned the birthday to Holly, figuring she wouldn't know about it in any case, but I had determined a great way to spend it if she would be willing.

"Would you be open to my coming to your school on Monday and sitting in on your class? I'd love to see you in action."

"Sure!" She was clearly happy that I wanted to do this. And then she asked, "Isn't that your birthday?"

I was touched that she knew and remembered. I confessed it was and that this would be a great birthday gift, witnessing her interact with the kids in her class. On my last day there, I spent the afternoon in her classroom, marveling at her skills and her gentle, supportive manner with her students, who were eating out of her hand. I took lots of lovely photos. It was indeed a great birthday. That evening we went to dinner and Danielle came with us. I flew home the next day feeling grateful.

I managed to arrange for Holly and Danielle to visit me the following year for a week in the summer. They arrived amidst a horrid heat wave, making tourist activities somewhat challenging, but we did take Danielle to see the local university both Holly and I attended. They met my husband-to-be, and we went shopping, something I yearned to do with them. We arranged for a group dinner and lots of family members attended and even a friend from high school.

"Why is he here?" asked Holly.

"Because he wants to know you," said I.

"He wants to know me, but my father doesn't?"

There wasn't much I could say to that.

I hoped these visits could become regular but the truth is, I have not seen Holly or her children since this lovely summer trip some four years ago. Much has happened in the interim. My father died unexpectedly, I was diagnosed with and worked my way through breast cancer and, when these crises passed, I got happily married.

Holly kept close via email and cards throughout my illness, which I found gratifying and helpful, but I was sorry to see the closeness ebb once I was well again.

Our connection once again feels strained, guarded, and tenuous. The door remains open but with no great ease do we reach through it to connect with the other. I sometimes grow weary of the dance. Other times I try to accept that she has received what she needs from me, and I need to let go. That's usually when I hear from her, something brief and noncommittal. I try always to keep the door open, even during those times of greatest frustration when I think, *Why is it so hard for us to bridge this gap?* And: *Forty plus years later, will she never tire of punishing me for surrendering her?*

It is said that many of us women tend to confuse love with longing. We are inclined to perceive the act of loving as yearning for someone unattainable despite the reality that longing is based in need or the lack of love. Did I actually love Holly's father or did I long for him, his love, his partnership and interpret these sensations as love? And what of my yearning for that baby that I gave away so that she could have a good home and so that I could avoid bringing her up in a toxic environment? Some days the answers seem clear. Some days they escape me.

The place I try to hold to is one of gratitude. While my surrender was painful, I offer thanks that I got to experience the power of giving birth—the thrust of new life, the energy expended by a new being entering our world. I give thanks for the chance to know Holly, even if that knowing is limited. I was spared a life of nothing but questions, with no answers, no understanding whatsoever of this person who came from my flesh. That this experience shaped my life is clear. Tenacity, a trait I ascribe to myself, surely has its origins here. Forced by circumstances to let go, it has ever since been difficult for me to do so. Most of the time I can resolve to accept the gifts that I have relished rather than to yearn for those I missed or at least presently seem to be denied. I am not without hope. I sense that chapters remain in this story, and I will do my best to rise to the occasion of their unfolding.

MOTHER STORIES
Ann Angel

Even as a little girl, I imagined growing up to be a mom in a big family. It would be much like the family of nine I grew up in, with noise and chaos and plenty of love. As a dreamy little kid who spent most of her time in a world of pretend, I created whole subdivisions from shoe box houses filled with cardboard furniture and paper doll babies. I dressed my Patty Page paper dolls in aprons. Princess Grace made a grand neighbor next door with the twins I drew with crayons and cardboard. Being a traditionalist back then, I gave Roy Rogers a briefcase but I let him keep his horse Trigger in the garage. As time went on, Barbie and Ken moved to the neighborhood. I created lovely stories for each family while dreaming of my own.

While I wasn't sure who my husband might be, I believed my story would be the one where I became mom to a dozen kids. I never saw that dozen, but I married my high school boyfriend and we became parents to four children.

Ours is an adoption story involving birth parents, some we know and some we don't. It crosses color and culture lines and, so far, spans a little more than thirty years. It has contained moments of crisis and grief, but mostly it has been filled with noise and chaos, and love and joy. While we've celebrated new life when we held each of our children and experienced the joy of birth, this has mingled with the sorrow of birth parents when our first granddaughter was placed for adoption. For the most part, this is the family I dreamed of and so much more.

The first moment I held each of my babies and breathed in that Johnson's baby scent on their hair and the milk scent on their lips I fell in love. I recall counting fingers and toes and admiring their skin and hair. My babies arrived with skin tones ranging from the color of burnt almonds to the palest of peaches. Although one was born with only pale fuzz covering his scalp, two others came into the world with wild curls framing wide green and brown eyes. One of my babies, the son with brown eyes so dark they look black, was also born with hair so thick we dried him off with a hair dryer after his baptism.

The first time I held each baby, I looked into her or his beautiful face and found myself falling into my dreamy imagination and writing their life stories.

"This one," I told my husband Jeff, after looking at Amanda, my firstborn with her serious eyes and heart-shaped mouth, "will be a thinker and an artist." With those watchful green eyes, she would surely do something creative and she'd teach others to do so too. I imagined she'd marry a man who loved her dearly and treated her well and she'd have a ballet school's worth of babies herself.

When my first son Nick was born, he proved a bit of a wild child with an amazing imagination all his own. He spoke to his stuffed animals about the stars and planets and would tell me they heard. As he grew, he took apart his toy trucks and trains and demonstrated insatiable curiosity with all things electric. I set his story at a drafting table covered with blueprints and wires. "He'll either be a pilot, astronaut or an engineer."

I told Jeff our third child, Joe, would give us many coffee-colored grandbabies and end up coaching or teaching little kids because he proved to be an affectionate, gentle and funny child. Our fourth child, a daughter named Stephanie, would be a modern dancer or anthropologist, maybe a zoologist. Or she'd work in television traveling the far corners of the universe. She was *so* active, amazingly curious, always seeking the unknown.

I look back and realize that the first moment I held them, I wrote their entire lives in my head. Each story was filled with love and accomplishment, dreams set in exotic places, and family and joy. It was most important that each story contain joy.

I believed, as parents, Jeff and I could love our kids so completely, the stories I dreamed would come to be. If I'm totally honest, I doubt I gave enough, if any, weight to the part of the story that began with birth parents. I tried to erase the reality that some, if not all, of my children's lives began with a less than joyful realization of an unplanned pregnancy. I had no idea that this unknown would weigh heavily on all our lives or how complicated that piece of the story could become.

Birth circumstances and adoption issues have colored the details of character and setting in unimaginable ways. These realities have created shifts and cracks and surprising twists as each of my children has grown to adulthood. Birth parents, even those we've never known, color the way my adult children look at the world and their place in it.

Joe's birth mother, who died shortly after giving birth, lives in my amazingly vivid dreams. In those dreams, she always asks about the son we share and reassures me he's growing into a beautiful man.

She always stands in a deep green rainforest on the furthest bank of a winding brook. A beautiful woman, with eyes and hair so vibrant they look blue-black: her characteristics clearly mark her as my son's mother. She combs her fingers through dark waves that cascade down her back. The first time she came to me, I stood on my side of the brook and watched her plait her hair, stunned by the scene. She looked into the water and somehow saw Joe's image reflected there. She asked, "Is that my son?"

She last held our shared son when he was six days old, only moments before she died. But since that first visit, she comes often to this creek in my dreams to look for him.

We talk about being parents and I fill her in on the details of his life. "He's playing basketball now," or "he's a kind and loving boy," or "a mischievous and funny teen." The last time I sat on the banks and

43

watched her across the water, I told her, "He has turned into a kind and hardworking man."

She and I have also talked across the creek's expanse about life and death. She told me what it was like to leave someone behind. She didn't want to die. In fact, she fought hard to survive. But she died of infection after giving birth on a straw pallet. She left three sons and a husband, farmers on a barrio deep in the mountains of Mexico. Joey is her fourth son, my second.

The first time she came to me, I was really sick. Afraid. After I had fallen asleep, or possibly passed out, my head splitting with pain, I thought the dream might be a warning of my own death.

"That's our son," I told her. "We named him Joey."

"He's beautiful," she said.

"He's wonderful." I glowed with the chance to tell her so. "Amazing, really." But I was sick and getting sicker. So I said, "He's scared because I'm sick and he's afraid I'll die. I told him I won't. Was I lying?"

She kept her eyes on Joey through the window created by the water. Her face filled with love and pride, and maybe a bit of admiration for our gorgeous boy.

"You won't die," she said and she looked at me for the first time. "One of us needs to be with him. He needs his mother."

His mother. I am his mother. But this story is complicated by the fact that she is too. Every time I consider that I have been given this gift, that I live as his mother, that I am the mother of four children through adoption, the idea of what this means astonishes me again. I raise our children for each mother.

I have told Joey about the mother dream and he always smiles, reassured that he has always been loved because his life contains me and his guardian mother.

Of my four children, Joey has this dream connection to his birth and my daughter Stephanie has a real connection through an opened adoption. But two of my children will probably never know anything about their birth and backgrounds.

Their beginnings seem empty holes.

It pulls sadly at my heart when I realize these birth mothers are missing their children's lives. But maybe they do know through some sort of spiritually connected way, just as Joe's mom can know.

Perhaps as I became familiar with the heft and weight of each of my children's tiny baby bodies when I held them for late night feedings, their birth mothers' arms grew heavy with the imagined weight. When I sniffed the citrus smell of my babies' hair after a bath, and the warm skin of their arms around me when they offered up hugs and kisses, did their birth mothers smell citrus in the air and feel the ghost of their kisses?

I know the salt of my children's tears when they've been hurt. Their smiles are intimate and their voices clear. Do their birth mothers dream of these things?

I have kissed away bruises and scrapes, calmed temper tantrums, sat through homework tears and chicken pox. I know the sweaty touch of their hands inside mine after scoring in soccer, volleyball, baseball, and even basketball games. For each event, I wonder if my child's other mother knew somehow, deep in her heart or soul, that this child had made another leap.

While I consoled a daughter who had discovered too late, at the moment she faced an audience with a violin perched in the crook of her neck, that it might have been wise to practice, I wondered if her birth mother felt the strings of her heart tug with sympathy. As I glowed with pride when my son who struggled with words once handed me an essay inscribed with an A, I wondered if his birth mother felt the wind of triumph beneath her feet.

Recently, I helped place posters on the walls as Amanda, a teacher now, organized her first classroom. I also just accepted compliments from Joe's employer, who said my son is exceptional for his kindness and care. Getting off the phone with Stephanie, now in college, I embraced the sweetness of her parting words, "Love ya, Mom." I smiled with pride when Nick got married, and was cautiously pleased to look over his first home purchase and even embraced his joy when he brought his first puppy to meet me.

Always, it seems, a part of my heart hopes that the other mother knows how wonderful her grown child is and how very, very grateful I am to be here. It almost sounds cliché to talk of how well-loved our kids are. But it's true; this is the tone of their stories.

I suspect I join the ranks of most adoptive parents when I say my children came from first parents who loved them enough to give them life. They have the fortune of growing up with parents who love them enough to raise them. In essence, adopted children receive life twice. That would make this story seem a fairy tale. But we have to live this to know how true it is.

And even then, there is the dark side.

Adoption professionals call it the primal wound. They're speaking in reference to the loss our children experience, often before they're a day old. But, even as that loss cuts our children, I find it has left its mark on our whole family.

While I've observed our shared children's joys, I've also borne witness to their sadness and loss. My heart ached for our married son as I reminded him he's lovable when his marriage failed. I worried that this loss would feed his primal wound.

While I coached my daughter through her own daughter's birth and stood with her when she turned her new daughter over to adoptive parents, I recognized that other mothers had experienced this loss for their children. Then I realized that this granddaughter's adoption connects seven mothers. These days I count our daughter's motherhood and add her baby's adoptive parents to the story of family.

This is the blessing and the emotional cost of adoption. Whether we're the birth mother or the adoptive mother, the tariff we mothers pay is the constant knowledge that we've created complex families and must trust that we can share mother love.

It weaves the thread of story for each of us in different ways. I feel I must do this mother thing well—very well. For me and for others.

And I fear I don't come close. While the abundant love that comes from adoption is amazing, the adoption toll for our children is that they might never know their origins, might never understand why loss had to occur before they became family. Even the daughter who knows her birth mother struggles with the idea of what might have been and what is. It appears she wants to know and love both of us, but doesn't always know quite how it all fits together. And I don't know how to help her. Neither, I suspect, does her birth mother, who is becoming my friend. For now, we hold onto those fragile threads of friendship; we share connections and worries about all of our kids, and we have to trust that it's best our daughter has us both. She will figure out how to weave these threads together.

When my oldest daughter, the same one who placed her daughter for adoption, searched and was told that her own birth mother didn't want to meet her, it felt like those threads had broken. But they're never really cut and I've learned I sometimes obsess on the "what ifs" that create a complete story. What if this birth mother never changes her mind and never gives our daughter the connection to her origins? What if she does? I realize the details are not mine to write; I may have to let go of completing this story.

My tow-headed son used to walk up to blond women, strangers all, and sit next to them to announce, "You could be my mother."

He fills his own lack of knowledge with wit, even humoring his older sister out of sadness at being refused the meeting by her birth mother. When she learned her home study had been the stuff of fiction—that the birth father with two or three other children apparently knows nothing of her existence although we'd been told he supported the adoption; that her birth mother's parents were kept in the dark although they'd been listed as being highly supportive of the adoption plan; that my daughter's existence must be kept locked away because this birth mother has a husband and family of her own now and doesn't want to rock her steady boat—my son asked if this meant parts of their lives were truly fiction. I told him yes. And he said, "You mean I'm not necessarily Norwegian? I could be anything I want?"

"I guess so."

He responded, "Today I think I'll be Korean."

Our oldest laughed along with him and then told me, "I'm just more yours now. I'm all of yours."

I knew then that this daughter has the power to spin these mother-threads into the story of her family.

If I could talk to each of my children's birth mothers, I would tell them I hope our children, whether they're ours by birth or adoption, all find a way to weave loss into the whole cloth of healing and connecting in our families. I hope their family stories always contain joy.

I hope each mother knows that she is welcome to meet our shared children. Meanwhile, I parent with my whole heart and then some for both of us.

Writers are taught not to use dreams to move their stories; it's trite to create an imaginative world and then have a character wake up to reality. My dreams walk firmly on the ground of reality though. My four children came to me through my own dream to have a family.

Adoption research bears out that it's part of an adoptive parent's job to support their children if they choose to seek and have relationships with their birth parents. It is in this way that we can help each of our children to let go of fears of abandonment. This is how they can grow into healthy adult relationships themselves.

After witnessing the huge sadness and grief an adult child of mine experienced when her birth mother turned down a meeting, I can't help thinking this birth mother missed out....

In the stories of my children's lives, there are no paper dolls or cardboard houses. But there are many mothers, and each birth mother is present in real ways. I see her in my children's voices and faces, in the way one might tilt her head when she laughs or another might giggle or laugh. I hope each birth mother knows that her love for her child fills my own heart. When these mothers come to me in dreams, I can sometimes hear sorrow and see loss. But when I catch glimpses of them in my children, I see their sweet innocence and love. I also see the joy of knowing each child's life is a life given and lived. While *ever after* hasn't arrived yet, each of us birth and adoptive moms can imagine the rest. It's a good story, really, a story built on hope, and one that weaves lives together through shared love. It is a story of joy.

REVISIONS

Natalie McNabb

CLARK ADOPTION

September 24, 2009

Oregon

10011 SE 12th
Suite 14
Portland, OR 97266
503-233-1009
fax: 503-258-2407
info@clarkadoption.com

Washington

Vancouver
360-993-5607

Spokane
509-844-7000

Montana

Bozeman
406-599-1040

www.clarkadoption.com

Dear Jennifer,

I hope things are going well for you.

I received a call from your ~~birth~~ daughter, Angela. As I am sure you know her birthday is right around the corner, and ~~this year is special since she is turning eighteen.~~ Angela is interested in opening her adoption.

Angela's adoptive parents recommended she call us to begin the process~~, but we must be mindful of the emotional turmoil they too will experience with this event~~. I met with them all a few days after Angela's call and met with Angela one week later. She is interested in ~~what you look like, where she comes from and hearing your version of the adoption story~~ learning more about you.

I know this may take time to digest ~~and that it may be scary and wonderful at the same time. You are~~

51

~~not alone, though. Millions are affected by adoption, and it does not end when papers are filed.~~ While you are considering your own needs and wants, I am here to answer any questions you may have.

Sincerely,

Linda K. Clark, MSW
Executive Director
lindaclark@clarkadoption.com

10/2/2009
Dear Linda,

I received your letter yesterday.

I would be happy to answer any questions Angela has ~~about my~~ ~~pregnancy, about Rob leaving. He slams the door shortly after my~~ ~~eighteenth birthday. My body slides down against the rusted fridge with~~ ~~its smell that not even baking soda, vinegar, bleach or ammonia can~~ ~~remove. I rest with my cheek against the kitchen linoleum and realize~~ ~~I haven't wiped under the stove since my stomach began to protrude.~~ ~~There's a Cheerio and a belly-up coffee bean I imagine looks much~~ ~~like I do. But, I feel more like the dust around the bean that softened~~ ~~its landing and cradles it now, the dust that will be wiped up after my~~ ~~stomach finally disappears. Rob runs off with someone who has shorter~~ ~~hair and a louder laugh. She loves popcorn at movies, barns, long drives~~ ~~and the countryside and hates skyscrapers and rush hour just like he~~ ~~does. I give birth at 2:37 am. I consider putting Rob's name in the father~~ ~~box on the birth certificate paperwork. FATHER UNKNOWN is all I write.~~ ~~We have nurses and social workers popping in and out, offering services~~ ~~for teenage mothers. "I'm 18," I tell them, "an adult. I'm fine." I want~~ ~~nothing but for them all to leave me alone. They say I look young for~~ ~~my age. One asks if I have postpartum blues. I turn toward the window~~ ~~and shake my head. They turn me loose with a wheelchair ride to a taxi~~ ~~that takes me to a friend's place. I struggle to feed you, but you can't~~ ~~latch onto my breasts. I can't satisfy your relentless need for milk. You~~ ~~cry, and my breasts and everything within me aches, wants to comfort,~~ ~~to feed, to nourish and to love. But, I can't. You cry and are only seven~~ ~~days old when my milk begins to dry up. You have to eat. I can't let you~~ ~~starve no matter how good they tell me breastfeeding is. I tell myself~~ ~~that I'm not into breastfeeding anyway, that I hate its public display and~~ ~~love the bottle's independence. For us, the bottle's best, and I plug your~~ ~~mouth with it. You eat ravenously and sleep in my arms while I stare. My~~

~~hands and arms tingle and go numb. My ache to nourish and love is not~~
~~quenched, but it dissipates within a few weeks. There is a void though~~
~~in its place. No happiness. No sadness. No anger. Nothing flows inside~~
~~of me. FATHER UNKNOWN on your birth certificate doesn't help us.~~
~~Rob resurfaces anyway, but without that girl with the louder laugh. His~~
~~parents push him for custody of you. "Considering your circumstances,"~~
~~they say, "and the mother's, it's for the best" and then take us to court.~~
~~"But she's my baby," I tell them, tell social workers and a judge. Each~~
~~takes a turn smiling, pretending regret. My lack of money, the pressure,~~
~~my youth and the emotional flat line begin to close in. Rob's parents~~
~~stare at me from across the courtroom as if they know what's best, as if~~
~~they can lead you somewhere I can't, as if they'd like to wipe me away~~
~~like dust that should not be near something so pure. I begin to believe it.~~
~~Rob and I opt for adoption by a couple we've never met instead. Angela.~~
~~Oh, my Angela. You were my baby, but my angel too late. Why does~~
~~regret only come after? I wonder what the world offers you now at the~~
~~ripe and wild age of eighteen.~~ Just let me know what I need to do.

Sincerely,

Jennifer

MOTHER BEARINGS
Colleen Harryman

The first years of my daughter's life found me consumed with hate in the hours before a visit from Jennifer, her birth mother. What on earth was the matter with me? After all, I was the diligent, considerate adoptive mom sending photos and updates of our daughter. I was the one who Initiated the phone calls for these visits. My God, it was Jennifer's sacrifice, her heartache that rendered my dream of motherhood a reality. Where was my gratitude? I was not worried Jennifer would take her daughter back. So what was it? The anger stemmed from something I could not or would not name.

Lucy's birth mother is intelligent, respectful, funny and loving. My husband Michael and I share many of her values and interests. Jennifer had graduated from our alma mater albeit in a different decade. Our views on religion and politics overlap as well. The three of us have often commented that we would have been friends under other circumstances. Under these circumstances, we are a family.

We met Jennifer on a Friday when she was eight months pregnant. She was open and engaging and we were smitten. The three of us talked so long that our social workers began to yawn and make less than subtle comments about the work day being over. To our surprise and hers, Jennifer went into labor that Sunday night. Her daughter was born at 3:21 on Monday morning and Jennifer wrote the name we had chosen, Lucy Erin, on the birth certificate.

As fate would have it, I was in a meeting that Monday and our social worker could not reach me. Michael, in the most wonderful role reversal, was the one to tell me that I was going to be a mommy. I started screaming and my female co-workers took up the call, knowing instinctively that a child had been born. Unable to hear what he was saying, I hung up with the father of my child to rejoice with the other mothers. At long last, I was one of the tribe.

Michael and I had both been adopted as infants. The adoption agency we had selected was the very same Catholic Charities that had facilitated Michael's adoption. We had chosen a domestic open adoption as Michael and I believed it better than the closed adoptions of our childhoods. We felt it necessary and beneficial for adoptive parents, birth parents and particularly adoptees to remain connected in some way. Fifty years of government legislated secrecy had engineered an abyss of grief for many if not all those touched by adoption. We reasoned that the more people who love and support our child the better.

As part of the adoption process for Catholic Charities, we were required to create a portfolio in which we shared our desire for a child and a snapshot of our lives through words and photos. It was, in essence, a marketing tool to be viewed by potential birth mothers. The first page of the portfolio was the "Dear Birth Mother" letter in which I wrote the following:

> We cannot tell you how much we admire your courage and selflessness. We are both adopted and have always felt extreme gratitude and love for our birth parents. Yet, we can only imagine how difficult this must be for you…As two very happily adopted people, we would like to thank you for considering adoption. Please accept our thanks on behalf of the birth parents we have never met.

The blasphemy of my words was made plain less than a year later when I, who had championed adoption to any and all, felt less than entitled to mother my daughter. My child's birth mother felt omnipresent and oppressive. Every parenting decision I made was in deference to my child's *real* mother. Logic held no sway in my overfull and bruised heart.

Petulant, I refused to clean the house the day before Jennifer's visits but would be up early the next morning, scrambling about and swearing as I worked to erase any evidence of maternal ineptitude. My husband did what he could to stay out of my way as he was an easy target for my churlishness. I would call friends in those early hours, dust rag in hand, mewling for absolution and wishing she did not have to enter my home. My animosity embarrassed and exhausted me. By the time Jennifer would arrive for brunch, I felt strung out having pitched about for hours in my self-created sea of anger.

Yet, each visit, miraculously, I was granted a reprieve. The moment Jennifer walked through our door my hostility evaporated. I could once again see the reality of this woman who was now part of our family. Jennifer had done the impossible and was willing to remain in her daughter's life and embrace it. Shamed and grateful, I welcomed my daughter's birth mother.

My anger refused identification for months until one Sunday, in the midst of pastry and fruit salad, I fell upon the twisted root of my ambivalence. Jennifer is what I would never be—my child's biological mother. It did not matter how many diapers I changed, hours of sleep lost, bottles fed, or tears dried. She radiated fecundity. In the face of Jennifer's beauty and youth, I felt aged. My barrenness underscored ironically, by my new-mother exhaustion. I was jealous and drowning in self-imposed inferiority. I could not believe I had such feelings. I, an adoptee married to another adoptee, had placed biology above all else; preposterous and true.

I was distressed at my inability to breastfeed. I fretted that my child would be sickly and stupid without that holiest of grails, lactating mammary glands. I began putting bovine colostrum in Lucy's formula upon the advice of a local naturopath. I felt an immense debt of gratitude that a four-stomached ruminant could give my daughter what I could not. I used cloth diapers and made all of Lucy's baby food with only organic ingredients. My house was cleaned with baking soda and vinegar. All of this did very little to assuage my feelings that I was inherently incompetent because I had not conceived, carried and birthed this wonder of a child.

Any parental misdeed—dressing the baby too warmly, a late feeding, or most grievous, an ungrateful thought about Lucy or motherhood—found me weighted with another stone of guilt. I knew that a biological mother would not err; a real mother would not pine for the days before parenthood. I destroyed a journal I had begun to record my journey into motherhood for fear of retribution from Jennifer, from Lucy, and from myself.

I find the entire adoption lexicon to be grossly inadequate despite the well-intentioned etymology of each term. Some birth mothers prefer to be called first mothers. I sympathize, as the term birth mother implies that labor and delivery is the mother's sole contribution to the child. Yet, first mother to me is apt when I think back to my early days of motherhood in which I felt every bit the second, serviceable but with obvious flaws.

When our daughter was two, I needed surgery. The day before, I asked my husband to take my picture with our daughter. I was scared. I wanted a happy photo for my girl in case the unthinkable happened. At the hospital, as my husband and I were walking towards patient registration, I sheepishly asked for one more favor. I asked him not to marry my child's birth mother if I were to die. My ungracious, irrational, insecure self presumed and detested the idea that Jennifer would inherit my life. I had convinced myself that her fertility made her more desirable than me, a whole woman with working parts. Given this, my husband would view Jennifer as the logical and oh-so-alluring choice for a second wife and mother to his child. I tortured myself with delusions of impending spousal betrayal.

Over time, I found my way through and around my jealousy of Lucy's birth mother. As my envy faded, my perception of Jennifer became clearer and more generous. I came into my own as a mother and realized that many of the things I did to foster and strengthen the connection between Jennifer and my daughter had also been done in service to the image I needed to project to the world. I wanted all to know that I was fine, more than competent, and that adoption was as valid as the biological path to parenthood. Yet I had not been fine. My child lost her first mother before I ever kissed her sweet face. I felt like I had blood on my hands.

We visited Lucy for the first time when she was four days old. She was in the care of a loving and dedicated couple who had been fostering babies for Catholic Charities for over twenty-five years. The walls of their home were covered with photos of all the children and families they had opened their hearts to over the years. Contrary to popular expectation, I didn't cry when I held Lucy for the first time. My immediate thought was, *There you are.* I may have even sighed. It was so difficult to leave her that evening. We were permitted to visit Lucy once a week for an hour and had scheduled our next visit before saying our first goodnight to our darling girl.

According to our social worker at Catholic Charities, the court date in which the birth mother agrees to and signs the Termination of Parental Rights (TPR) is scheduled about six weeks after the birth of a child barring any complications. A birth mother may change her mind at any point prior to signing the TPR. Jennifer's court date took place eleven weeks after Lucy's birth.

During this legally mandated waiting period, Michael and I were at odds with ourselves. We wanted to be parents. We had fallen in love with our daughter and Jennifer. However, we were also two adoptees who had never met their birth families. Neither of us knew if we could bear the separation of another mother and child. The decision was never ours to make, and yet we struggled with our guilt and our desire to call Lucy our own.

It has been said that when one becomes a parent, the ghosts come out of the nursery. I have also read that adoptive parenting is very much like biological parenting but with an extra layer. I think my nursery ghosts took layering to new heights. After my envy faded, but before I could permit Jennifer to be herself, I placed her in the mother of all roles. My child's birth mother became positively archetypal, an unwitting stand-in for my own birth mother and for all birth mothers.

I had been steeping and stewing in adoption books that contained phrases such as "primal wound" and "ghost self." My identity and my own beginnings competed for my attention as I worked to be the best damn (adoptive) mother ever. I gave required reading lists to grandparents, aunts, uncles and Jennifer. It is true that I wanted our family to be on the same page and available should Lucy need help as she grows. However, it also true that I was desperate to make sense of my own experience. I wanted answers from Jennifer that she could not possibly give me.

One spring morning, Jennifer stopped at my house after a "special person" breakfast at Lucy's school. Jennifer was going to borrow one of the books from *the list*. We greeted each other warmly and I asked about the breakfast. Then, without warning, I began sobbing, telling Jennifer that she IS Lucy's mom (too) and that I wanted HER to someday have the every day experience of motherhood and that she IS part of our family and how sad I was for all that she went through. The poor woman had not even made it into our living room.

I imagine all of this was a bit much for Jennifer given that she thought she was picking up a book and returning to work. Jennifer had known me for five years at this point so my tears and urgency weren't news. Standing part way in my front door, Jennifer comforted me: the maternal figure reminding me that she was not going anywhere and that we had our whole lives to help Lucy grow into a healthy, happy adult. As embarrassed as I am by my behavior on that day, I am still moved by the sense of peace Jennifer was able to instill in me. She had said the words I longed to hear from that other birth mother; she was not going anywhere.

Visits with Jennifer are now much anticipated events. We do not see her as often as we would like nor as often as we used to. However, she is always there when Lucy expresses the need to see her birth mother. Jennifer has gone to Lucy's school functions and attended many birthday parties. As a result, she knows our family and friends and they know her. We are fortunate to have this level of openness and closeness. It is always hard to say goodbye.

What I cherish about these visits is the opportunity to watch Lucy and Jennifer interact. They have different eye and hair color but the thickness of their hair and the shapes of their faces and their eyes are the same. They share mannerisms, movements, and interests; I take all of it in greedily and happily. I cannot get enough; for most of my life, I have not had that biological mirror and it's a marvel to me. I am happy that Lucy will have that reflection as she grows. I am thankful that Jennifer is strong enough to be that mirror.

It is amazing to recall the drama of Lucy's adoption process, given the quotidian nature of our lives today. I liken it to the amnesia that follows childbirth. Jennifer is now free to be herself; the ghosts have receded. I pray that Jennifer was never aware of my duplicitous feelings. Who is to say that Jennifer was not experiencing similar things? She has never shared her feelings about all of this, not directly.

Several years ago, the three of us spoke at a Catholic Charities orientation for adoptive parents. When asked about her experience, Jennifer said that, to her, this is fate. It is her belief that she brought Lucy into the world to become our daughter. Perhaps she's right. I don't know. What I do know is that the adoption triad is indeed a triangle much like the one off the coast of Bermuda; the boundaries are hard to discern and it's easy to lose your bearing.

As a new mother, I desperately wanted a map of the maternal to guarantee that I would not make any mistakes, cross any unacceptable lines, make any messes. I sought the counsel of fellow mothers only to discover that there is no map but many directions. My compass, I realized, was my own heart and my own mistakes. In the end, it is simply time and the daily act of mothering that have done what all my good intentions and countless parenting books could not: made me a mom, who, on most days, and with varying degrees of grace, embraces the ambiguous nature of parenting and of life.

MOVING CLOSE

Robin L. Flannigan

"We're moving to Buffalo."

I look up from the glass candleholder I'm admiring on the coffee table and stare at Jessica blankly. I don't know whether I'm more surprised at the sudden announcement or at the way I'm feeling about it. She goes on to say that her boyfriend has been accepted at the University of Buffalo, an hour away, and she's moving there with him to work at a nearby Cheesecake Factory and start classes at Erie Community College.

"Really?" is all I can think to say.

Jessica, my daughter's birth mother, is 24. On her 21st birthday she went out on a dinner date but felt too nauseous to eat much. Turns out she was pregnant. She wasn't sure what she wanted to do with her life, but she felt she wasn't independent or responsible enough to parent a child—"The idea of being a mother at my age was absurd," she'd told me later—and she wanted to finish her education. She'd been taking courses on and off at a community college around the corner from her house. Besides, she could tell her relationship with Peter wasn't going to be permanent. They'd become exclusive five months earlier, after flirting during shifts at T.G.I. Friday's, where they both waited on tables. She had different values, and no piece of her wanted to try to make things work for the sake of their unborn baby.

Two days after giving birth, standing in my living room with Peter at her side, Jessica placed Annalie in my arms during a private ceremony to acknowledge her strength and the commitment my husband and I had made to raise her baby the best we could.

Our adoption contract promises Jessica may see Annalie, who has her birth mother's delicate fair skin and quick wit, two times a year but we always more than double that. Jessica comes over to celebrate Annalie's birthday in October and a late Christmas in January, though Annalie is much more interested in whisking Jessica from the front door to her playroom than in unwrapping presents. On warmer days we head to the beach to bury our feet in the sand and watch Annalie's daring stunts on the playground; once when Jessica shot her a nervous look, Annalie, trying to reassure her, said, "Don't worry. I'm very advanced for my age."

We all attend a Birth Mother's Day celebration in May, the day before Mother's Day, as well as our adoption agency's annual picnic in July.

Occasionally Jessica and I give some sort of joint public presentation on open adoption. I remember feeling particularly insecure during one of the earlier ones, when Annalie was just beginning to toddle and I'd been wrestling with a similar unsteadiness in my role as her mother. Speaking to a group of prospective parents, I admitted to the sometimes emotionally daunting task of maintaining relationships with two other families (we also keep in touch with Peter) while trying to forge my own.

When it was Jessica's turn, she talked about how, when she sees Annalie, she doesn't think about the baby she held in the hospital. Instead, she's immediately taken with a confident, happy child who is right where she belongs. In that moment, I realized Jessica has enough strength for the both of us.

Patrick and I decided to work with a nontraditional adoption agency in southern Vermont, five hours from our home in Rochester, partly because it was started by a hippie and operated at the time out of a creaky old house. Three months after we finished all the paperwork, our caseworker from the agency called to say a birth mother wanted to talk to us.

Patrick took the call while I was shopping at Target. When I pulled into our driveway, he was standing on the back porch, waiting to share the news. We spoke to Jessica by phone Monday night. We met her and Peter on Wednesday after work; they both live in the area, so we invited them to our house. We were matched on Thursday.

Annalie was born three weeks later.

When I first heard about open adoption, the concept sounded a little threatening. Until then I had endured years of medical procedures and failed pregnancies to have a biological baby, and I feared that sharing our child with someone else, even the person responsible for making us parents, would disrupt the ideal family we'd been trying so hard to create. But over a long lunch with a social worker who had two children of her own through open adoption, several things became clear. This was not about us, this was about the baby. It would be a blessing for our child to be exposed to the heart of a woman strong enough to make such an agonizing decision. And our daughter would always have immediate access to any questions about her identity. After that lunch, Patrick and I agreed to an open adoption without much discussion. It just seemed right for us.

Others weren't so certain. More than once we fielded the question, "How can a woman just give away her baby like that?" We tried to answer patiently, explaining that birth mothers are ordinary people who find themselves in extraordinary circumstances. They place their babies—they don't give them away—out of an unfathomable love, hoping to give them the life they wish they could.

To me, of course, Jessica is no ordinary woman. She made me a mother.

She was the first to show our daughter what it means to be selfless. I cried with pride when Annalie surveyed every one of her toys to make her first donation, offering up one of her biggest baby dolls for a stranger who didn't have one. She'd placed the doll in a plastic bag, patted its belly and said, "There, now you'll be safe."

I share these sorts of anecdotes with Jessica often. Sometimes because I feel I owe it to her, but mostly because she makes it easy.

Jessica laughed at the story about the time Annalie, then 2, was playing with my makeup and I remarked that the colors weren't her best, that we have different skin tones.

"You have Jessica's skin," I told Annalie.

She held up her forearm, observed it for a few moments and scrunched her nose, as if wondering how someone else's skin had gotten there when she wasn't looking.

I held my forearm against hers. "See? Mine is darker. You have light skin just like Jessica does."

That seemed to clear things up enough. She reached into the cosmetics bag, rolled on some gloss and smacked her lips.

Other anecdotes have been more serious. Driving home on a recent afternoon, I was telling Annalie, now 3, about something that had happened before she was born.

"Was I growing in your tummy?" she'd asked.

"No. No, you weren't."

I could've left it at that. It was a perfectly factual answer. I turned onto the exit ramp by our house and came to a slow stop at the light.

"You didn't grow in my belly, sweetheart," I said, craning my neck to see her expression in the rearview mirror.

She was looking out the window, contemplative. After a few moments and several stops and starts, she declared that a friend had been in his mother's belly.

"Yes. Yes, he was."

The light turned green and we made a wide left turn around a big truck.

"Do you remember whose belly you grew in?" I asked.

"Jessica's."

I smiled and praised her correct answer, then left it at that. She knew enough for now.

More questions will come, some more complicated than others. With Jessica's support, we'll answer them.

We are in this together.

But she's moving away. This boyfriend is a serious one. We'll still get together more than our contract says we must, and she'll be back in Rochester frequently to hang out with her parents and friends, which will make it easy to coordinate visits. Then why do I feel so unsettled?

I guess it's because being able to run over to Jessica's apartment, where she's just broken the news about her move, is a bonus. Her birthday package had come back to us marked as undeliverable, so I'd called her up and made arrangements to stop by with it between appointments, after picking up Annalie from nursery school. You can do that when you live less than two miles away from each other.

We can't do that when she lives in Buffalo.

And what about the other impromptu get-togethers? Like the time Annalie and I ran into Jessica's father in the grocery store parking lot. He said he was meeting up with her for dinner at a nearby park, so I shortened my list of errands and accepted his invitation to join them.

The truth is, the relationship I have with Jessica, though unexpected and uncharted for each of us, has, more than any other, taught me about the power of the human spirit, in particular its capacity to accept, on both our parts, the things it cannot change.

When I explain to people why my husband and I chose the open adoption route, it always comes down to this: we decided to embrace our reality.

We're teaching Annalie to do the same, and Jessica is helping us.

We're all finding our way, and I suppose I know deep down that once she moves, this extra distance—small as it is—won't really matter in the grand scheme of things.

Jessica's family. No matter where she lives.

A Wing and a Prayer

Maureen Ciganek

"Nowllaymedowntosleeplpraythelordmysoultokeep . . ." The speed
at which Daniel recites his prayers reflects how wound up he is tonight.
Impulsiveness creeps into every aspect of his daily routine.

Standing beside Daniel's bed, I shift my weight from one foot to
the other. I stare down at my son. He is sandwiched between teddy bear
patterned sheets and an assortment of stuffed animals, with his hands
clenched palm-to-palm atop his comforter.

"Slow down and show God some respect," I say, trying to hide my
irritation. After dealing with Daniel's bedtime antics for the last hour, I
don't need a gas gauge to know that I'm running on fumes. I hope to
land on my own bed down the hall soon, before I crash.

"Angelsguidemethroughthenightandwakemewiththe
morninglight." Daniel takes a deep breath and slows his pace for the
improvisational prayers that come from his heart. "God help me have
good dreams—not bad, sad, mad, mean, violent or dying—none of that,
and help me not to be scared. Help me be good, listen and obey. Help
my birth parents get lots of money—cha ching—for healthy food, and
milk and juice. No junk food." Lifting one hand, Daniel uses his pointer
finger to draw a circle in the air with a diagonal line through it. He looks
at me watching him.

"That means no junk food."

"That's what I thought. It's like the no smoking symbol."

"Yeah." He smiles at my acknowledgement and continues with his
prayers. "God take care of my relatives across the world and help my

grandparents here live forever. Thank you for my life and for my family. Amen."

"Amen."

No matter how battle worn I get from our daily tug-of-war power struggles, I listen attentively to Daniel's prayer variations each night. His prayers give me a fleeting glimpse into the core of his armor-plated soul. One night several years ago, he offered up this prayer: "Dear God, how was your day? Good, I hope. Someday I'll take over for you—when I'm dead." The words still resonate in my mind. That is Daniel. He wants to be all-powerful, in control, and he's here on earth to impose his will on my husband Richard and me.

Once in a while, when I'm especially frustrated with Daniel's controlling behavior, Richard reminds me how Daniel recited the *Our Father* to him when he first learned the prayer: "Our Father, who art in heaven, hallowed be my name. My kingdom come, my will be done, on earth as it is in heaven." We laugh every time Richard tells the story. "Thy will be done" is a concept our son struggles with when it comes to taking directives from adults.

Turning in bed, Daniel hugs an armful of stuffed animals to his chest and fingers the soft binding of his blanket with his left hand while sucking the thumb and pointer finger of his right hand. I pull the covers up and tuck them around his neck to ward off the autumn chill. I kiss his cheek and smooth his silky black hair. This is the only time of day when Daniel allows me to snuggle him and kiss him and show him affection without protesting. Some nights he even lets me rub his back.

"Mom," Daniel says when he is settled comfortably in bed, "when I was little did my birth parents wave goodbye?"

His question catches me off-guard. An image of a dark-haired man and a dark-haired woman waving goodbye while baby Daniel is carried away by a nurse or social worker flashes through my mind. I ache for my son and the parents he never got to know. I am struck by the profound loss Daniel experienced as an infant. Blinking back tears, I consider how to answer his question. Keep it simple, honest.

A Wing and a Prayer

"I don't know. We never met them."

"I had a dream they were crying for me."

I study his face. He's trying to be stoic but his eyes fill with moisture. I think about Daniel's birth parents. Where are they now? Are they healthy? Do they have food, shelter and warm clothes? Do they have other children to care for? Do they believe in God? Do they hear Daniel's prayers? Do they pray for him? I wonder. I wish I had more information about them to share with Daniel. His birth parents are a mystery to us, yet these two people became part of our family when we adopted the child to whom they gave the gift of life.

"Were you dreaming about them the other night when you had a nightmare?"

Daniel nods. "I don't want to dream about my birth parents. It makes me sad." His dark eyes penetrate me.

"You're home, you're safe with us." I tuck a few stray animals around him. "I'm thankful you're here—that you're our son." I want to wave him off to dreamland on the wing of an angel with the knowledge that he's safe and wanted and loved. I kiss his cheek once more.

"I love you," I say, turning out the light.

"I love you, too."

"Sweet dreams—I'll see you in the morning." I head for my bedroom.

"You too." Daniel's words trail behind me.

After getting dressed for bed, I go out to the living room to say goodnight to Richard.

Lounging in a black, leather recliner with his feet up, he is mesmerized by the news headlines glowing on the screen of his laptop computer.

"I finally got Daniel to bed. I'm going to bed, too."

"Okay. Goodnight."

"Don't stay up too late."

"I won't," he says without lifting his eyes from the computer.

I'm too tired to care about his inattention right now. Besides, I wouldn't be able to tell him about Daniel's defiant behavior after school today anyway, because Daniel isn't asleep yet and, from his room, he can hear everything we say. There have been nights when Richard and I are discussing the events of the day and Daniel joins in the conversation, yelling from his bedroom. Who, what, when, where, how, why—he interrogates us, demanding to know what we are talking about.

"It doesn't concern you, now go to sleep!" I yell down the hall. I've learned to go into his room to see if he's actually sleeping before discussing anything important with Richard.

In the warmth of my bed, I lie in darkness and listen to the wind whistle outside. I imagine the leaves dancing on the air as they fall from the trees. Soon it will be November 2nd, the eight-year anniversary of the day we flew to Slovakia to adopt Daniel. I go back in my memory to the evening when, a few hours after our arrival at the airport in Kosice, we stood with Jon, the lawyer who facilitated the adoption, at the door of the orphanage. It was a damp night, around 6 pm. The streetlights behind us illuminated the gray door, and leaves fell around us while we waited for a response to our knock. A nurse dressed in a white uniform holding a small, black-haired child opened the door. I was stunned by the child's beauty. His dark hair brushed the tips of his ears and the bangs covering his forehead framed large brown eyes. The nurse smiled at us as we entered the foyer of the orphanage, then she spoke a few words in Slovak to Jon, turned, and vanished down the hall.

"Was that Daniel?" I asked Jon.

"You're not allowed to see the children without the approval of the orphanage director," he replied.

"Richard, do you think that looked like Daniel?" I persisted in vain.

"Could be. That little boy is much cuter than the photograph we have of Daniel though."

The next day Richard and I sat alone with this same beautiful little boy in a playroom at the orphanage. His birth parents had named him Daniel. He lay between us on a red tumbling mat, tummy down, sucking

72

on his right-hand thumb and pointer finger. Richard and I looked at one another and at Daniel. I rubbed Daniel's back. We were strangers to this twenty-six month old child, and the comforting words we spoke were in a language he didn't understand. This perfect little corduroy-clad boy, the answer to many of our prayers, was right in front of us—and all I could think about was what we were getting ourselves into by adopting him. A wave of fear and uncertainty rushed through me. I couldn't share my thoughts with my husband for fear he'd say, "This was your idea in the first place."

"Do you want to play?" Richard sprawled on the floor in front of Daniel and rolled a blue plastic car one way and another in an effort to engage him. "Vroom, vroom, vroom!"

Daniel's eyes followed the car, but his body remained in place on the red mat. He was content sucking his fingers while I continued to rub his back.

Eventually, with a little patience and a lot of coaxing, Daniel warmed up to us and we held him, kissed him, and played with him until he was wound up like a spinning top. He communicated with us using giggles, pouts, and baby talk. He didn't speak much Slovak, but Richard got him to say the word auto.

Here we were, with the little boy who would soon become our son. There was no turning back—it was meant to be. Whatever the future held for the three of us, we would handle it together as a family. This was part of God's grand and mysterious plan. Thy will be done.

I wake to the sound of dishes clattering in the kitchen. Richard breathes deeply beside me, still sleeping. It's dark outside but Daniel must be up already. I jump out of bed and rush to the kitchen, hoping he's not making a mess. "You're up early. What do you want for breakfast?" I ask. Daniel kneels on the floor looking at the cereal boxes in the cabinet next to the sink.

"I want Fruit Loops," he pouts.

"We're out of that. How about Cinnamon Toast Crunch?" I try to sound convincing.

"I'm sick of that. I want Fruit Loops."

"We'll get some on the way home from school. Would you like instant oatmeal instead of cereal? You like Apple Cinnamon, or we have Peaches and Cream." I'm hoping to avoid a full-blown tantrum on a school morning. I don't want to be late for work. Fortunately, Daniel decides he'll eat Apple Cinnamon oatmeal—two packs. Whew. I dodged an encounter with the anti-aircraft artillery hidden just beneath the surface of our lives.

We navigate our way through the rest of Daniel's morning routine without incident. Eat, get dressed, brush teeth, comb hair—no—okay, leave the hair sticking up. Each small act involves negotiation, a dance to determine who is in control at any given moment. And each small act has the potential to become a large-scale battle, complete with venomous language, yelling, screaming, kicking, biting, spitting and flailing around on the ground. Child-rearing experts advise parents to pick their battles wisely, but with our son, each breath we take has the potential to set off an explosive chain of events.

Daniel has Attention Deficit Hyperactivity Disorder (ADHD) and a mood disorder. Both of these disorders also fall under the umbrella diagnosis of Reactive Attachment Disorder (RAD). It's possible some of Daniel's problems are genetic, but we don't have any information about his birth parents' medical histories. However, Reactive Attachment Disorder stems from early childhood trauma.

Daniel spent the first two years of his life in an orphanage where he was one of many little bodies that needed feeding, changing, and comforting. During this time, Daniel's brain became wired without the benefit of a mother's hand helping to guide the many colored wires of his formative experiences into their proper positions on the circuit boards. The wires of his early life experiences—which include those for trusting adults to care for him—are mixed up and mismatched. Without consistent input from a significant, nurturing caregiver, Daniel's brain developed wiring patterns that serve his primal needs of self-preservation and survival. As a result, it's difficult for him to trust adults, especially parents, to do things for him and he has a compulsive drive to be in control. A master of manipulation, he does what he can to satisfy his needs and wants.

When I leave for work, Daniel is watching TV, waiting for Richard to get ready and take him to school. "Have a good day, you two! Daniel, I'll pick you up from the after school program around 4:00 today."

"Okay."

Closing the door, I hear Daniel yell at Richard, "Hurry up—tick tock!"

At work I immerse myself in the activity of teaching art to elementary and middle school students. Paper, pencils, crayons, markers, scissors, glue, paints, brushes, clay—I shuffle these and other supplies while students periodically shuffle in and out of my room changing classes. I have no time to think about Daniel—until I sit at my desk and check my email.

In the brief seconds before my email appears on the computer screen, my body tenses. I haven't received a note from Daniel's teacher for over a week now, and I'm lulled by the thought that maybe Daniel is behaving and, after a rough start to the school year, perhaps he's settled down and he'll be fine. He'll cooperate and focus and be on task in class. He'll control his incessant chattering and impulsiveness. He'll be okay. I shouldn't worry.

It's 1 pm when I receive not one but two emails from Daniel's school. The first note is from Mrs. Connelly, Daniel's teacher:

> *Daniel has been having a difficult time adjusting to our class routine. I've been journaling his behavior to see if his meds need to be adjusted and, often, there's no rhyme or reason to his behavior. He was playing with things in his desk, so the principal brought in an open-bottom desk so he doesn't have materials to play with. Yesterday he got a detention for using inappropriate language in gym class. He has been very argumentative and combative with me. Also, yesterday he was going to take his*

*scissors from his pencil case to the after school program and I
told him he couldn't. He yelled at me and told me I have no right to
his backpack and said he would have me put into custody by the
police.*

Every muscle in my body is knotted. I think about last year when
Daniel gestured to his teacher with his middle finger and told her he
was going to kill her. Each negative report from school prompts another
phone call to Daniel's psychiatrist to discuss possible adjustments to
his medications for ADHD and the mood disorder. Finding effective
medication for Daniel's problems is an ongoing trial and error affair.

I click on the second email. It's from the principal of the parochial
school. He and Mrs. Connelly are at a loss for how to handle Daniel's
behavior, despite all the suggestions and information I've provided.
They would like to meet with Richard and me.

We've been summoned to the principal's office. As a mom, I'm
embarrassed and frustrated by my son's behavior. As an educator, I'm
empathetic toward Mrs. Connelly—it's hard to teach with a disruptive
student in class. And the part of me that still responds to authority like
a ten-year-old girl is worried about getting in trouble because of my
association with the naughty boy. What will people think?

I reread the two emails several times, trying to take in the gravity
of this situation. Is there a possibility we'll need to move Daniel to a
new school? Would his social, emotional, and educational needs be
better met in a public school where there are teachers who specialize in
working with difficult children?

By the time my next class enters the art room, I am wiping the
corners of my eyes and blowing my nose, but it's too late to hold back
the tears. I've taken a bad hit. I go into a tailspin and have to leave
my students with their third grade teacher in order to pull myself up.
Therapists tell us not to take Daniel's behavior personally, but I'm no
Flying Fortress.

When I pick Daniel up after work, he tells me tall tales—no, no
problems in school. In the grocery store, he throws a tantrum over the

purchase of Fruit Loops—he wants candy instead. At home he flaunts a defiant attitude regarding homework—it sucks. Throughout the evening he randomly hurls choice names at Richard and me. I can't wait until his bedtime. It's one of those days when I wonder what a one-way airplane ticket to Slovakia costs now.

I try to imagine what Daniel's day would have been like if he was still at the orphanage or if he was with his birth parents, but I can't imagine either scenario. When the thought that he could have been adopted by another family enters my mind, I suddenly feel fiercely protective of my son, and I realize Daniel's where he's supposed to be—with us, his parents. Thy will be done. However, at this moment that doesn't comfort me much.

While Richard's in the kitchen and Daniel's in the living room watching TV, I sit on the Rubbermaid stool in the bathroom and cry. The bathroom door is closed for privacy, but it's not long before I hear a knock and Richard peeks his head in the room.

"What's the matter? Are you okay?" The light from the living room silhouettes Richard's figure.

"I've had a rough afternoon. I got an email from Daniel's teacher and the principal of his school—they want to meet with us—and Daniel's behavior has been bad since I picked him up after work. I'm really worn out tonight." I sniffle and blow my nose in the already damp clump of Kleenex wadded in my hand.

"What happened at school?" Richard sounds worn out too.

"I'll tell you later, when Daniel is asleep," I say, blotting my tear-streaked face with the Kleenex wad.

"Okay, well, dinner will be ready soon," he says and shuts the door.

A few minutes later, Daniel comes into the bathroom wanting to know why I'm crying.

"I'm sad about your behavior—I wish you could control yourself better." My voice is unsteady and my face is wet again.

"I'm sorry." He hangs his head and leaves the room quietly. Within seconds, he returns to my side and hands me his large Winnie the Pooh bear. I cuddle the peace offering in my lap while Daniel stands and rubs my back. I am moved by this gift of empathy, but I am also aware that it's only a matter of time before I witness another display of sassy behavior. It's hard to know how much control Daniel has over his own behavior, and how much of what he does is due to his wiring.

Tonight, I make sure Daniel is sound asleep before I tell Richard about today's drama. The computer is off, so I have my husband's undivided attention. Sitting in matching leather recliners, separated by a small table piled with books, we talk and talk and talk and shake our heads in frustration. We discuss the option of sending our son to another school, but we'll meet with his teacher and the principal before making any decisions. Both of us want Daniel to get a good education, but we also want him to behave in school. We wish we knew how to best help him. We wish we had the answers to solve his problems. We continue searching for answers—often in vain—but we keep trying to help him because he's our child.

Before going to bed, I go into Daniel's room. The night-light casts a soft glow, illuminating our sleeping son. His head rests comfortably on his pillow, haloed by a bevy of stuffed animals. Brownie, Night-night Teddy, Beary, and his other beloved teddy bears and stuffed animals are all accounted for while he dreams.

I am amazed at how peaceful Daniel looks when he's sleeping—as if he doesn't have a care in the world. I kiss his sleeping face, readjust his covers to keep him warm, and whisper in his ear, "I love you, beautiful boy."

In my bed, too exhausted to sleep, the events of the day replay in my mind like an old movie. The song "Coming In On a Wing and a Prayer," popular during World War II, provides background music. The chorus swells with hope: "Tho' there's one motor gone, we can still carry on, Comin' In On A Wing And A Pray'r."

Sometimes when my engines are failing or completely disabled from battles with Daniel, the only way I can carry on is on the wing of a guardian angel and the whisper of a prayer. "Thank you, God."

Pictures of the Day I was Born
Molly McCaffrey

Part of me wishes I could go back, back to the time before I met my birth mother. After I found her, she insisted on visiting as soon as possible and came bearing gifts—a t-shirt from the bar and a gold necklace with a pendant In the shape of a horseshoe: beams of light surround a crowned gold heart. It reminded me of pictures I had seen of the sacred heart of Jesus, and I couldn't help but wonder what it was that I believed in. I don't wear gold. Just silver. But how could I tell her that?

After my birth mother left, the first thing I did was call my mom. My real mom. That's what I call her when I have to distinguish between them. There's my real mom, and then there's Barbara, my birth mom. But usually I just call her Barbara.

"I can see everything for what it is now," I said to my real mom on the phone.

"Really?" she said. "What does *that* mean?"

"I was worried that I would feel conflicted. That I wouldn't know who my real family is. I used to feel guilty about it, but it's not the same anymore. Now I know that you and Barbara are two different parts of my life, and that's all right."

But as soon as I hung up, the guilt returned. I felt like a traitor. I wanted to call my mother back and tell her that I would never to talk to Barbara again. I wanted to tell my mother that I love her, that she's the only mom I need. I didn't realize how transparent I was being until my husband asked me what's wrong. I could feel him circling, searching me for clues, but I didn't want to give in to his interrogation so soon.

"What did your mother say?" he finally asked.

"You know what she said. The same thing she always says."

"Let me guess. She *said* she was fine with Barbara being here this weekend. She *said* it's no problem at all, but you can tell it bothers her?"

I didn't respond. I didn't have to.

Dave knew he was right. He knew my family as well as I did, and he'd heard our story over and over. My younger sister and I were both adopted before we were six weeks old. Like kittens. Just old enough to be weaned, but not old enough to remember. Except we're not from the same litter. In 1970, I was born in Baltimore, the illegitimate daughter of a student nurse. Her ex-boyfriend Dan had returned from Vietnam not long before I was conceived but said he wasn't ready to start a family when Barbara missed her period. After she let me go, I spent a month in a Catholic orphanage before meeting the two people I would come to know as parents.

My sister Katie has also met her birth mother, but her story is still more of a mystery: her mother Marie was only seventeen when Katie was born in 1973, and her upper-middle class parents pressured Marie into giving Katie up for adoption. On Katie's eighteenth birthday, Marie filed the paperwork to find out who had adopted her daughter. Less than a month later, she received the information in the mail and called our home. Years later, Katie and Marie's relationship is still tenuous—crafted out of rambling e-mail messages, awkward phone calls and short visits. To this day, nobody knows, or is willing to admit, who Katie's biological father is.

My parents never hid the fact that we were adopted. Before I was old enough to read, I was able to recite by memory the story of how I came to be their daughter. And they always said that they would support us if we wanted to look for our birth mothers or any other family.

They said it, but I never believed it was true.

I believed, instead, that doing so would be uncomfortable for all of us, that it would hurt. So I never thought about it in any serious way. Searching simply wasn't an option. I was at least *that* devoted to my parents—devoted enough that I wouldn't even consider the one thing I was afraid would truly wound them.

"So what are you going to do?" Dave eventually asked me that night, and I realized I should do something.

"I don't know," I said. "Maybe I'll e-mail her. It's too late to call back." It occurred to me then that e-mail was actually the best option. It would give me the chance to go over some of the details we didn't get to on the phone, and it would allow me to do so without having to deal with any more of my mother's endless questions.

Dear Mom and Dad,

I just wanted to let the two of you know that everything went great with Barbara this weekend. Besides feeling a little like I wanted to throw up while I waited for her flight to come in at the airport, it was smooth sailing. I really can't believe how easy it was.

Yes, she looks a heck of a lot like me, and we have much in common. Barbara talks as much as I do, she's just as open as I am about everything (she's totally fine with the adoption and how everything has gone—it's amazing how well-adjusted she seems), and she also tends to lose track of time and run late like I do.

On the other hand, it looks like I got my desire to plan everything in advance from Mom. Barbara was content to wing it, but I kept hearing a little voice in my head saying, "What are we going to do next?" Dave and Barbara practically had to tie me down to the sofa.

Well, I guess that's all for now. Hope you are doing well. I'll talk to you more soon.

Molly

I considered signing the e-mail "Love, Molly" so that they would know how much they mean to me, especially since one of my worst fears was that they would read Barbara's visit as an attempt to replace them. But since I'd never signed my messages that way before, I also worried they'd find it unusual. Would they think I was acting strange? Or worse yet, would they see it as an attempt to alleviate my guilt? And wasn't that exactly what it would have been?

The truth was that I have never been the kind of person who signs messages with the word "love" or relies on predictable sentiments to express my feelings. In that way, I was more like my dad, so ultimately I opted to leave it out, instead trying to simply be myself, which until then had always been easy.

Barbara married my biological father, Dan, one year after she gave me up. The wedding took place six months before their second child Danny was born. Dave likes to joke that the two of them had yet to figure out where babies came from. After Danny, Barbara and Dan had three more children: Ben, David, and Terri. So we're all fully related. Not half brothers and sisters, but the real thing.

The adoption agency found Barbara eight months before her visit, mere weeks after I had filled out the necessary forms and passed the required psychological tests. It was during one of those interviews when the issue of my birth father first came up. I was told to prepare for the possibility that Barbara might have reunited with him. These things happen, they said. So I was aware of the possibility, even if it made me rather anxious. But when we found out for sure, the shock hit my husband Dave hard, as if he never really understood the whole thing was real. Suddenly, I had more family than he did. Overnight, or thirty years later depending on how you looked at it, I had inherited an entire brood.

I met Dave in college. We lived on the same floor in the dorm but didn't hold a real conversation until I was wandering through the lobby looking for strangers to photograph for my photojournalism class. We had only been introduced a few hours earlier—Dave's grip firm enough to impress me when he shook my hand—so I figured he would still qualify as someone I didn't know. At the time, he was sitting with his friend Dexter, who I would later find out was the most candid person in our dorm.

Dexter's interrogation started immediately. "What do you want to take our picture for?" he asked me.

"It's for class. I'm supposed to take portraits of strangers."

"But you met me three hours ago," Dave pointed out.

"I won't tell if you won't," I said.

I shot an entire roll of film while we talked, careful not to let Dexter know that three-quarters of the photos were of Dave. As I worked, I told them about the class: "My professor said that some of his students have met the person they will eventually marry while shooting this assignment. As soon as he said that all I could think about was how something like that would never happen to me."

"For all you know," Dexter said, "you two could end up married someday." He looked at Dave and then at me, connecting us with an imaginary line.

I blushed and stood up, moving away from the table where the two of them sat.

"I think I have plenty," I said, holding my camera up as an explanation.

"Don't let him intimidate you," Dave said. "He's just compensating for his own insecurities."

Dexter was skeptical. "As if," he said simply, but I still felt a sense of relief pass over me. I had always wanted to find someone like Dave, someone who wasn't afraid to say what was really on his mind, but I never thought I actually would. The strange thing was that, even that first day, Dave sensed this about me. He tuned into my apprehensions as readily as most guys tune into a football game.

"Don't talk to any more strangers," Dave advised before I left. "They say it's dangerous."

Sometimes I think Dave has always known me, sometimes he even knows what I want before I do. Like with Barbara. Dave had wanted to know where I had come from before I could put words, or even thoughts, around my yearning.

"But aren't you curious?" Dave asked me when I first told him I was adopted.

"Not really." We were eating dessert when the subject came up. I swirled my spoon around the mess of chocolate chip ice cream in the bowl in front of me while I considered his question. I really wasn't curious about my biological mother, but I also wasn't ready to admit any more than that so I said, "I guess I never thought about it."

"You never thought about it?"

He sounded skeptical so I tried to explain. "I have a great relationship with my mother. We talk about everything. I don't lie to her like some people do. It's not always easy, but it works. I don't need another mother."

Dave leaned back in his chair. He was just barely nodding his head. It was as if he was taking in what I had said, trying to find some new angle. Finally, he said, "But what if you're an heir to some great fortune? What if you're a Kennedy?" He paused before continuing. "Don't you want to know?"

Dave would speculate this way for hours, but I knew his interest was deeper than just wanting to know if I was entitled to a large inheritance. Slowly, carefully, his interest in my past became my desire to find Barbara. But, at first, the inclination was his. Before Dave, this was the one question I was always afraid to ask.

Barbara looked like me, stood like me, and talked like me but, even after she had come and gone the first time, I felt as if she were as odd and unknown to me as any stranger we could have picked up at the airport that day. And for all of our similarities, she was nothing like I had imagined she would be.

When she got off the plane, she was wearing a lavender-colored cotton twin-set with dark violet flowers embroidered on the surface. Her hair was shorter and less kinky than mine, but it was exactly the same shade of brown: the drab color of day-old tea highlighted by accents of washed-out gold. I did not inherit her muddy brown eyes, but I fear that the deep lines that crawl across her skin like flesh-toned spiders will someday be mine. My wrinkles aren't as pronounced as hers, but they *are* there, even if they're not yet visible to a less critical eye. As soon as I saw her, I knew that in twenty years I would look just like she did.

Back at the airport on Sunday morning for her flight home, she protested as she took her glasses off for one last snapshot: "You'll see my wrinkles."

I pretended that I didn't know what she was talking about. We stood under the artificial lights of the terminal, smiling, an arm around each other like we were old friends.

Later, driving back from the airport, Dave told me that it was strange to see someone who resembled me so much. I knew that his words meant more than he was willing to admit. I was pretty sure Dave wasn't comfortable with the idea of Barbara once she was a real living person and not just an imaginary character we dreamt up as we lay in bed trying to fall asleep. Maybe it's because Barbara and I are so physically similar. In one picture from that first visit, we look like a perfect match. Just like one of Barbara's sweater sets. Maybe Dave was afraid that knowing Barbara would make me more like her. I'd start getting wrinkles and wearing mom jeans.

And yet, I couldn't help but wonder if all of the guilt and anxiety I was feeling at that time was Dave's fault. Maybe, if it hadn't been for him, I never would have looked for Barbara.

Maybe I would never have wondered who I really am.

When I was a kid, I didn't think about it much—being adopted. My parents told me it meant I was special. They told me that only someone who loved her child more than herself could give her up, and I believed

Silent Embrace

it was true. I told other kids that I was special, that my parents had paid for me. When my parents cleaned out their basement one summer, they actually found a receipt from my adoption, and I discovered exactly how much special costs. At two hundred dollars even, I was a bargain.

I used to fantasize about who my birth father might be. When I was little, I watched the *Dukes of Hazzard* and imagined that John Schneider was my long lost dad. Then as a teenager, I started to believe it was Art Garfunkel. Finally, before I found Barbara, I had settled on Bob Dylan as the most likely possibility. The only requirements seemed to be that he have curly hair and be famous.

I never fantasized about having a birth mother. In fact, just the idea of such a person made me uncomfortable. By the time I started daydreaming about my unknown father to "Bridge Over Troubled Water," I was smart enough to know I fantasized about birth fathers because my own father wasn't around as much as I would have liked.

I only saw my father in pieces while I was growing up, and most of our activities revolved around the things he liked to do: we would jog, fish, or play basketball; we would go to the library; and we would visit the dog pound. The pound was the only one of those places I actually longed to visit, and dogs—especially down-and-out, needy ones—were an interest my father and I shared. So on Saturdays, we would go to the city-operated animal shelter. It was as dirty and pathetic as you would expect. The stale smell of urine and the super-potent toxicity of industrial cleanser worked in conjunction with the high-pitched howls of the abandoned dogs to give me a headache that would often take hours to shake. As I walked along the cages, I tried not to think about the idea of numbered days, and, for the most part, it never bothered me. Now it seems obvious that this look-the-other-way type of behavior was something I learned from my father, but at the time I was oblivious to how he dealt with this cruel reality. I was so happy to be with him and

86

so eager to adopt a pet that I could look past the small imperfections during our time together.

Sometimes we would walk one of the dogs. It was on such occasions that I would give in to my emotion and end up in tears, begging to take the animal home while my father led me quickly back to the shelter to return the miserable little pup.

Despite my many pleas, we never did get a dog from the pound. My mother was worried about poorly trained or rabid dogs, and she didn't care for mutts. She wanted a purebred, and eventually that was what we got.

After Barbara's visit, I thought about the dog pound and couldn't help but wonder why we went there so often if my father knew we would never take anything home. I would have asked my parents for an explanation, but I already knew what they would say. My father wouldn't respond, hoping to avoid a real conversation if he could, and my mother would say I think too much. She'd tell me that my father took me to the dog pound because I liked it—simple as that—and that I should worry about important things, like my career. I'd eventually interrupt her with more questions, and finally she'd retaliate by telling me I push too much, attacking me where she knew it would hurt most.

My whole life, my family has accused me of overthinking things, of interrogating them without reason, and it has always been a sensitive subject, especially since they were the ones who taught me that good relationships were about communication. But when push came to shove, they wanted me to reveal myself without asking the same of them. Rather than admit this, though, they accused me of pushing people to their limit.

"You never give people a chance to finish, Molly," my mother said to me on the phone mere hours after we'd dropped Barbara off at the airport. "You are *always* one step ahead of people, finishing their sentences for them and going on to a new thought."

"I didn't do that with Barbara. I'm not like that with everyone. Just you. You're family."

"Well, aren't we lucky?"

Dear Molly,

Your dad says hello, and we are both happy for you. You are at a perfect age and maturity to handle meeting Barbara now, and I am glad it has worked out for both of you.

We already know from what you have told us about Barbara's letters that she has many qualities and talents that you have inherited. She has an ability to feel comfortable around people. She is thoughtful and creative. One thing I would like to ask . . . has she ever played the guitar or a musical instrument? Oops, I think that was Katie's mom.

Molly, I am really glad Dave is with you for support. This is an important time in your life. Relax and enjoy it. It will be over sooner than you want it to be. And yes, there will be many questions that you forget to ask. A lifetime cannot be reviewed in a week end. Enjoy Barbara and cherish her and her family.

I hope her flight home was a good one.

With lots and lots of love,

Mom & Dad

On the phone tonight, I told my mom that meeting Barbara has made me realize that I'm too hard on them, but all I can think when I read this e-mail is that weekend is one word, not two. And that it's typical for my mother to get my sister and me mixed up. All my life I thought that it was *my* biological mother who played guitar. No wonder I could never carry a tune.

Both my sister and I wanted to take piano lessons when we were young, but my parents said they couldn't afford it. We had a four-bedroom Colonial with a landscaped yard and an in-ground swimming pool, my dad was a vice president at Johnson & Johnson and we vacationed at the Jersey Shore, but for some reason we still couldn't afford a used piano. After much persistence, Katie and I finally convinced my parents to let the two of us enroll in piano lessons on a trial basis. For six weeks, we trudged a block up our suburban street to practice what we learned on a piano at a neighbor's house. When the trial period was over, my mother kept promising to work on my father about getting a piano, but nothing ever came of it. Except that I can still do scales, and because of all the money they saved, my parents are enjoying a comfortable retirement in Florida.

Barbara turned out to be the opposite way with money. She told us during her visit that she gave my biological brother Danny a thousand dollars to buy a car and that, at the age of twenty-four, my other brother Ben was still living at home. After college, my parents told me that they expected me to get a place of my own, and even though they never said it, I knew I could never ask for money. They claimed that people who gave their kids money did them a disservice, and they cited a cousin who'd lived off his parents his whole life as evidence of this. Of course, it's at times like these that they always fail to remember that my grandfather bought my mother a brand new yellow Karmann Ghia convertible when she graduated from college. My father sold that car after they were married as if it were a piece of extra baggage he couldn't wait to dump.

Money is not the only thing that's different between our families. I was a stellar student, but Barbara's kids—my four brothers and sisters—have all been diagnosed with learning disabilities, problems that have to do with things like hyperactivity and not being able to pay attention. I wonder how I escaped. Or if I really did. My mother's words come back to me over and over again: *You are always one step ahead of people.* I wonder about having such a gift. At times my brain feels like it's on speed, racing ahead of me at an unwise rate of travel. Maybe thinking fast is more of a liability than an asset.

In school, I was always in the gifted and talented classes. I suppose that means that I often did well on tests, that I never worried about being stupid and never believed it when people said I couldn't do something. I failed freshman comp my first term in college, but I never felt like a failure. I never even contemplated such a possibility. Instead I did as little as I had to do to get an A the next semester. Although I was educated enough to know that bad grades didn't mean I was dumb, I'm not sure they tell this to kids with learning disabilities or kids who grow up without money, and I can't help but wonder how my life might have been different had I grown up in Maryland with Barbara and Dan.

When I found out that Barbara and her kids were all jocks, I was at a loss. Katie had always been the athletic one in our family. But the only two people in my entire biological family to attend college went on athletic scholarships. I still can't figure out how that makes sense given everything they say about DNA and the nature-versus-nurture debate or even, more simply, what it means about me.

"Do you like country music?" Barbara asked me on the second day of her visit.

"Not really," I said and regretted it at once. I wondered if I was I supposed to lie.

"Oh," she said, and then she paused. I'm not good at pauses. I like to fill them up with words. Everyone knows this about me. Well, everyone who knows me, and I realized then that Barbara didn't really know me at all. I feared that I had hurt her feelings irreparably because I didn't want to listen to songs that twang. I let myself imagine that our relationship would end before it ever really got started. But then she spoke again: "I was just wondering because we have karaoke."

I looked at her, not sure what she was talking about. The word karaoke tapped on my brain like a knock-knock joke.

"At the bar," she added, as if she knew I was confused.

90

"Oh, yeah." I had forgotten about the bar. Their bar. The family business. I told myself to pay better attention. Barbara's husband Dan, my birth father, and his mother ran the place. Even though it's called Daniel's Restaurant, food is an afterthought, and it mainly appeals to bikers because—thanks to an irresponsible grandfather clause—they can pull their motorcycles up to the outdoor bar and have a beer without ever leaving the leather seats of their bikes. Everyone in the family puts in time at the bar: the kids all have regular shifts, Barbara's sister works on weekends, and Barbara pitches in for big events. To my surprise, I also found out that Barbara was employed by the hospital where I was born for over thirty years. Like a criminal returning to the scene of the crime, she worked in the maternity ward, helping to deliver the babies of others.

"We have it on Tuesdays and Thursdays, and we all get up and sing." Barbara was still talking about the bar, but I was having trouble focusing. *Knock, knock. Who's there? Your mom. Your mom who? Your mom who sings karaoke.*

"Do you sing?" she asked.

"No, I can't sing at all," I said. "Never could." My next thought was that it was strange that the person who had given birth to me was able to sing well enough to perform in front of a crowded bar. With that realization came another one: maybe Barbara wasn't my biological mother, maybe there had been some mistake. But before I had time to fully consider that option, I looked at her face and saw the truth: no one has ever looked like me before, and Barbara could have been my twin. I wasn't sure whether I should be relieved or disappointed.

"Are you a good singer?" I asked her.

"God, no!" She blushed as she spoke and chuckled a little to herself. "I'm a horrible singer. But I don't care. I just get up there and do it. We all do."

Later she showed me pictures of the karaoke-singing family from Maryland. She told me they all get up and sing "Family Tradition."

Together. It sounded to me like the von Trapps on moonshine, and I hoped my distaste didn't show on my face. After she was gone, Dave laughed and said I'd almost surely have to join them when we visited. I didn't laugh with him because I couldn't fathom how I would get out of it.

Before we met, Barbara and I talked on the phone. She sounded different long-distance than she did in person. I didn't have the face, the body, to go with the voice. All I could go on was what I heard. I had photos, but they weren't a living, breathing being, so it was her voice that gave me a moving picture. I saw a teenager, young and awkward, nervously tripping over her words. The picture was wrong. She's the opposite of that—she's sure of who she is and comfortable with it. Solid. A delicate rock. As we ate breakfast during her visit, I listened to her words echoing in the air in front of me and recalled my original picture of Barbara. Her voice sounded gravelly because she had just woken up. Mine does the same thing in the morning. I was surprised again at how many of our different pieces seem to match. Every hour I noticed something new. I wondered if other people notice these things all their lives.

> *hey molly,*
> *i just wanted to say hi real quick before i run off to class. my mom (your mom too!) is flying to see you today. i am sure you are aware of that. don't be too nervous. there is absolutely nothing to worry about. i am going on a road trip to charleston, south carolina to see my boyfriend romas. i am very excited. he said that it is in the upper eighties there so i am taking my bathing suit. have fun with my mom and take care of her. i am sure you two will love the time you spend together. i will talk to you when i get back. good luck.*
> *love,*
> *terri*

92

My biological sister Terri always writes "love, terri" at the end of her e-mail messages. She only found out that I existed eight months before Barbara's visit, but she has loved me online ever since. I don't even say those words to my real sister Katie or my mother. I tried to ignore it at first, hoping she wouldn't do it again. But she did. *Every* time. Finally, I gave in. Now I sign my messages the same way. I feel as if I must.

I bought birthday cards for Barbara to take back to my biological brothers Ben and David. I reluctantly signed their cards "Love, Molly." It was two months after we started dating before I put such a declaration in writing to my husband, and yet I found myself doing so with two strangers. I worried that, like me, they would find the salutation overly effusive, that they wouldn't know that Terri had started it, that it was just a family thing. Then, I asked myself—they are family, right?

Terri called twice during Barbara's visit. The two of us had talked on the phone before, but that weekend her voice—like her mother's but younger, more boyish—sounded strangely unfamiliar. So when I heard her voice, I passed the phone away quickly, as if it were diseased.

Despite my contact with Terri, I avoided Danny, Ben, and David— my three biological brothers—completely those first few months. I'd never had any brothers, and I didn't know how to do it. I felt sure that there was some trick, some secret brother language that I had yet to learn.

They're not like any of the men I know either so my relationships with other men didn't really help. In the pictures Barbara sent me, they wore wool ski hats and plaid flannel shirts, and thick dark whiskers covered the pale skin of their jaws. They looked as if they could beat somebody up. They looked like they just had.

When I first saw the pictures, I was shocked. I expected to see six people who looked exactly like me. They were my flesh and blood after all. But when I saw six people with different bone structures and different eyebrows than mine, all I could think was, *Why don't they look more familiar?*

Now, I know what to look for: Ben's eyes, Terri's smile, Danny's forehead. And even though I look exactly like Barbara did at my age, it took me a while to see even that—as if I were blind to my own likeness. I hadn't yet figured out what I share with Dan, my birth father, but I hoped to soon. I had expected to see a mirror image, but I finally figured out that it's all the pieces together that make the picture whole.

Right around the time I started looking like a woman, my father began treating me differently. I had a huge growth spurt when I hit puberty and, by the time I was thirteen, I looked more like a co-ed than a kid.

I clearly remember when my father first took notice of how much I had changed. It was the night of my eighth-grade graduation, and I was wearing one of my mother's old dresses. The knee-length skirt was shimmery and blue, and it followed my curves just closely enough to draw attention to them. My father watched me walk in the room, looked me over appreciatively, and told me I looked all grown up. For weeks, I wore his approval like a precious jewel, but after that, it seemed like he was at work more and more. Dave always says that he imagines the hardest time for a father would be when his daughter begins to take the shape of a woman, that he too wouldn't know how to relate to a child who is developing breasts and becoming desirable to other men. I understand what he is saying—I even believe it—but that still doesn't completely make up for the time we lost.

Dan, Barbara's husband, gave her a red rose wrapped in plastic to pass along to me during her stay. I suspect that it came from a gas station they passed on the way to the airport. I've never liked red roses, but I try to appreciate the thought. Unlike Barbara, Dan hadn't written me, and he hadn't called. It was almost as if, to him, I still didn't exist.

When I talked to my mom after Barbara left, she was quick to bring up the one part of the visit I didn't want to talk about: "Did Barbara ask if you were mad at Dan?"

I *was* angry with Dan—still am—but I didn't want to admit it to my mother. I was angry with him for breaking up with Barbara when she got pregnant with me. It felt like he abandoned her, like he abandoned us really. But I knew that my anger had never really been about simple rage. It was about fear and apprehension.

Barbara told me that the night before her visit, Dan said he wasn't sure if he was comfortable with her coming to see me. She told him that he didn't have much choice in the matter.

I was surprised that he hadn't mentioned his hesitation until the night before she left. When I asked Barbara about it, she said Dan wasn't very good at being open with his feelings. Then I remembered something Terri had said in her first e-mail. She said that she didn't think her dad would know what to say if he ever met me. Remembering that made me feel even more panicky, more edgy—the same way you feel when you have to get a shot.

"I'm not mad at him anymore," I said in answer to my mother's question, knowing I'd already told her this at least twice. "I forgave him the second Barbara told me he felt bad. There's no use being angry with someone who knows he screwed up. He feels lousy enough."

"Okay," my mother said. I wasn't sure if she was hearing what I was saying, which made me want to change the subject.

"You'll never guess what Barbara's first car was," I said.

She paused to think, and then in an energetic voice began to say the name of her first car: "A Karmann—" she started but stopped before she had completed her words.

"Yes, a Karmann Ghia!" I said, forcing myself not to wonder why she had hesitated mid-sentence. "Isn't that weird?" I said, determined to smooth over my anxieties. "You both had the same car."

"Hers must have been used." My mother's delivery was hot and short, her words came through the receiver like spitballs.

"No," I insisted, trying my best not to lose my patience. "She went to the dealer and bought it herself. She said she made payments." I said words that I knew to be true in an attempt to convince her, but somehow I still felt like I was losing. "She had saved up," I added, fabricating new material to strengthen my case, thinking somehow it would help.

"You *can* buy a used car from the dealer," she said. The anger had gone of out her voice. She sounded complacent, as if she knew she had won.

After we got off the phone, Dave asked what my mom said about the Karmann Ghia even though he knew the gist of it before I answered him.

I didn't want to admit my mother's shortcomings out loud. I told myself that it was all right that my mother said those things and made such haughty implications. I told myself that that was how she made herself feel better. Then I wondered why she needed to make herself feel better. And the feeling of guilt came back to me all over again. And, for a second time that night, I wished Barbara's visit had never happened.

My mom has a lifetime of memories with me. Good memories and bad memories, happiness and resentment. Thirty-nine years of me, for better or worse. That's a lot to brag about. The only thing Barbara has that she doesn't is the day I was born. And obviously I don't remember that.

Barbara took pictures, though. Pictures of the day I was born. I'm quite a bit smaller than I am in any of the five-week-old baby pictures my parents have. I hardly have any baby fat yet, and my skin is the color of bubble gum. At first I thought it was odd that there weren't any pictures of Barbara, but only pictures of me by myself. When I asked about this, Barbara just looked at me without saying anything, and then I realized that, of course, she had been alone.

You weren't supposed to take pictures, Barbara told me but admitted she didn't know that until she'd already done it. She said she couldn't believe how much I looked like her when I was born. "None of the others looked that much like me," she said. And she's right. I've seen their baby pictures too. But that's all she has that my mom doesn't. That one day. And that's when I realized she now had a whole weekend too.

Barbara left a card behind. Snuck it into our bedroom when I wasn't looking. Dave was in on the plan. I opened it after I e-mailed my mother. My name was written on the envelope, and there was a little flower drawn next to the scripted letters. The card had a picture of Monet's "Pond Lilies" on the front. I had already noticed how well Barbara picked out cards. They featured famous works of art or quote well-known writers.

My mom gives me cards with glitter. You'd never know she's the one with the college degree.

Dear Molly,

Every day I offer a silent prayer of thanks that such life was placed in my hands and that now I am being blessed with the miracle of touching even a part of it.

I felt that perhaps this early birthday gift would be a gentle reminder to you of how much I treasure the gift of your life and hopefully the friendship we will share.

Happy Birthday today and everyday.

Love,

Barbara

It's the gold necklace. I can't help but think *if only it were silver.* I could wear it every day. In the car on the way back to the airport, I complained to Barbara about how my mother can never pick out gifts for me. "She doesn't understand what I like," I had said. But when I found the gold necklace, I felt like a traitor. Barbara didn't know me any better than my mom. The cards were just a fluke.

Barbara used the word "blessed" the same way my grandmother does: "We are so blessed," Grandma always says. My real grandmother, that is.

Dan's mom didn't even know I existed. Barbara told me that when Dan broke up with her after she got pregnant, he never told his mom what had happened, and even with Barbara coming to visit me, he still hadn't worked up the courage to tell his mother the truth. In her mind, that weekend was not unlike any other—she thought Barbara was at a nursing conference. She had no idea that her daughter-in-law was meeting the child she and her son had given up thirty years before.

Dear Molly,

We've been thinking about you and did try to call you once. I hope all is going well for you and Dave. I know your birth mother is coming to visit soon. It will be an emotional experience, and I will be anxious to talk to you. But no matter what, you belong to us.

We love you very much. Have a great visit and a very special love to Dave too.

Grandma & Grandpa

P.S. Get something you'd like from us for your birthday.

My grandmother's words were the ones that stuck with me after Barbara left. *But no matter what, you belong to us.* She sounded so sure of herself. So proud. I had worried that Barbara's visit would cause doubts for everyone in my family, but my grandmother was unshaken. To someone who didn't know my grandmother, her words may have seemed possessive or proprietary. But I knew she said it only because she was confident about who she was and what family meant. If only she could have cleared it up for me.

I didn't see either my mom or Barbara on my actual birthday the year of Barbara's visit. My parents were in Florida for the winter. They're retired, and they like to joke that they are spending my inheritance. My birthday was two weeks after Barbara left, but she told me that I was born thirteen days late. It's no surprise since I clearly inherited my tardiness from Barbara. As we hurried down the airport corridor to her gate only fifteen minutes before takeoff, she joked about how she couldn't remember the last time she'd been to a flight so early.

After Terri called, Barbara tried to figure out if Terri was ovulating.

"I don't think Terri and Romas are sleeping together yet," Barbara said. "At least I hope they're not."

I was silent. I thought maybe Barbara would know what that meant. But she didn't know me well enough yet to read my signals. She didn't know I only keep my mouth shut when I don't want the wrong words to come out—I knew Terri and her boyfriend Romas were sleeping together, and I knew Terri was on the pill. She had said as much in her e mail messages.

"We get pregnant easy in this family," Barbara added with a laugh.

"Really?" I imagined myself with a basketball underneath my t-shirt.

"I got pregnant with Danny while I was on the pill."

When I told my mother about Danny's conception, she said, "You have got to tell Terri."

"Why?" I asked.

"She could get pregnant too. She has to use a condom." My mother's plea sounded rather frantic, and I wondered why she was so invested in Terri's ability to procreate.

"I don't think that's the kind of thing I can e-mail her, Mom." I tried to imagine how that would go.

Dear Terri,

I know this is going to sound strange but your mom told me today that she got pregnant with Danny while she was on the pill so I told my mom, and she said you should use a condom even though you're on the pill. Hope you are having fun in South Carolina with Romas!

Love,

Molly

Barbara made it safely back to Maryland that night. She called after I had talked to my mother. She said that I should fly out to see them soon. I reminded her that I don't fly and, just like I do with my mom, said, "Remember?" before I could stop myself.

I couldn't sleep after I talked to Barbara. Instead I lay in bed wondering about all the changes that had just taken place. And when the clock hit three am, I realized that Dan, my biological father, would just be driving home from closing the bar, reminding me again how different my life had been from theirs.

The gold necklace sat in a blue leather box on the table next to the bed. I could see the outline of it in the dark. It reminded me of the rosary my grandmother bought me at the Vatican. The clear glass beads came in an ornate green and gold case that I carried with me everywhere, clinging to it like a life jacket when I used to fly. They say the Miraculous Medal will protect you from fatal harm. Over time, the gold and green paint wore through, revealing a dull grey fabric, but still, I carried it. Then one time during takeoff I realized I had forgotten it. I closed my eyes and prepared for the end, but nothing happened. After that, I stopped going to church.

I wondered then if the blue box would have the same fate. I thought I might carry the box with me since I knew I'd never wear the necklace. Like a talisman, I imagined it protecting me. Or maybe it would help me understand.

Dear Molly & Dave,

Thank you for a wonderful week-end. It was all I expected and more. I feel like we've known each other for years. The two of you seem to share a special relationship. Continue to grow as the unique individuals you are, and I'm sure you will continue to grow in love as one. Be good to each other and love tenderly.

God bless.

Barbara

P.S.—the money is for all the phone calls.

Barbara's thank you arrived a week later. "Shit," I said out loud when I saw the word weekend split in two. A twenty-dollar bill fell out of the envelope.

"What's that for?" Dave asked.

"Phone calls."

"How many phone calls did she make?"

"Not twenty dollars worth."

"It's our inheritance," he said.

"I blame you for this mess," I said, but I couldn't help but smile, and then I thought about what that word meant—inheritance. It made me wonder if I would ever be a mother. And if so, what kinds of things would I leave behind for my children? What would I have to give them? I imagined myself writing a letter to my unborn daughter on her thirtieth birthday. The letter would say things like, "Hope to see you this week-end. Love, Mom." And there would be a pair of silver earrings tucked inside the envelope. My daughter would let out a breath of disappointment at the sight of the sterling jewelry, thinking woefully about how she only wears gold.

32 CEMETERY ROAD
Emma French Connolly

Even though thirty-eight years had gone by, we arrived early. The meeting was to take place at 1:00 pm. We pulled into the parking lot of the church where we were to meet just before noon, so we drove back to a Starbucks we had noticed earlier and got coffee, trying to pass time. I couldn't sit still.

Thirty-eight years of dealing with emotional detachment, all those years of therapy, had suddenly come loose.

"We need to go back to the church," I said to my husband, Robert. "What if they get there before us and leave?" The day was cool and hazy, serene even, but I hardly noticed, as I was deep in thought.

I began to think of the King's Daughters Home for Unwed Mothers in Natchez, Mississippi, at 32 Cemetery Road, and the memories I had left there. For thirty-eight years I had suppressed a multitude of feelings so deeply that no one, especially my own soul, had any idea how my dissociation with the event had impacted my life. But dissociating with the event was the only way I could survive it.

Robert understood my anxiety.

When Robert and I realized we had a serious relationship back in 1998, I told him my birth mother story. We married the next year. In 2002 we made the three-hour trip from Jackson, Mississippi down to Natchez, to that house at 32 Cemetery Road. That visit was the only time I had returned to the house in all those years. The house, originally built in the late 1700s, was high on a bluff just outside Natchez overlooking the Mississippi River. I will never forget the day Robert and I went back to that house, because the structure seemed smaller than I remembered it, as childhood things often do. A rusted chain link fence surrounded the property and a locked gate prevented us from driving up the long driveway. A small and weathered square stone marker had sunk deep into the soil near the road. The numerals 32 were chiseled in each side. The house looked abandoned. We climbed over the fence. Robert had thought to bring a camera. I had mixed feelings of excitement and fear as we went up on the front porch and looked in the windows. Old wicker chairs, once painted dark green, sat on the porch and were covered in spider webs. We shaded our eyes and peered in the windows. I recognized some of the furniture—especially the long wooden dining table where fifteen pregnant girls had shared meals. We went around to the back of the house and found an unlocked door—as if someone knew we were coming. Robert called out, but the house was empty.

We wandered through that old house, and into the very room where I had stayed those many years ago, and the memories flooded my brain and heart. I remembered looking out the same window at the same scene—graves as far as the eye could see.

Downstairs in the room that had been the house mother's large paneled bedroom there remained a huge safe. I guessed that's where the records were kept. On the windowsill in that room was a key with a tag that read "King's Daughters Maternity Home." I picked up the small key and dropped it in my pocket. That key became a metaphor for the secrets held deep in the hearts of all the girls who stayed at 32 Cemetery Road—I wanted somehow to set them free.

There were rules about getting mail back then. Everyone was supposed to be anonymous, so we were introduced by our first names. The practice was silly because everyone told their last names. Each girl was given a number. To receive mail, the writer must have addressed the envelope to a girl's "secret" number, at 32 Cemetery Road, Natchez MS. If our names were on the envelope, the house mother was instructed not to give us our mail.

I had come to 32 Cemetery Road with nothing but a small suitcase, and I left with an overwhelming sense of emptiness. The house possessed a rich history that I would only learn about in later years while trying to find my daughter, who I had given up in February 1968.

In 2003, I returned again to Natchez to research the history of the King's Daughter's Maternity Home. As I looked at old newspaper clippings in the county library, I found photos of the house mother who worked there during 1968. In the library file was an old brochure advertising the Maternity Home. In an article about the home, I also discovered that the house had been a home for wayward women for many years in the 1800s and early 1900s. How interesting that it became my home for a time as well.

Robert was out of town when I received the call from the caseworker that April morning in 2006, four years after we made that visit to 32 Cemetery Road.

"Are you sitting down?" she asked, after identifying herself as calling from the Mississippi Children's Home Society.

I sat down. "Now I am," I answered, my heart pounding. I already knew what she was going to say, but I wanted to hear it. I wanted to hear the truth. That my daughter, whom I had given up for adoption, wanted to find me.

Alone and silently, even though I had no idea where she was, I had marked every milestone in my daughter's life: at the likely age she started school, graduated high school, got married, gave birth to her first child—hoping that as she grew she would begin to wonder about me and desire to know me, who I was and why I had to give her up.

As early as 1969, I had begun the search for her. First, I called the Mississippi Children's Home Society and a caseworker said it was too late, that I had relinquished parental rights and there was nothing I could do except perhaps add information to the "file" of the adoption record. The same person approved my writing a letter to my daughter and said the Society would reveal my name and address if my daughter chose to look for me some day. I did not give up.

In early 1975, I put the following classified ad in the Jackson Clarion Ledger and in small town newspapers in several Mississippi cities and rented a post office box for replies:

> SPECIAL NOTICES
> Birth mother searching for daughter
> born 2/27/68 in Natchez and given up
> for adoption. Confidentiality assured.
> Reply to . . . .

I received no responses.

By 1987, I had divorced my first husband, John[1], and I was a single parent with three young children.

While browsing the local newspaper in the early 1990s, the Dear Abby column caught my eye. There was information about a mutual consent adoption reunion organization, International Soundex Reunion Registry, located in Nevada. This non-profit registry was founded in 1975 by Emma May Vilardi and "Dear Abby" highly recommended the agency. The address was printed in the column and I sent in my ten-dollar donation. About a week later, I received a notice that I was registered. I continued sending in donations for years afterwards, hoping my daughter might be searching for me as well, but I received no replies from adoptees.

After I got my first personal computer in 1991, I began searching for birth parent/adoptee reunion sites over the Internet and posted a message on every one I could find. Most matches occur by birth date, gender, and birthplace. My usual posting on adoption search sites was the same: "Birth mother searching for daughter born 2/17/68 in Natchez, Mississippi."

In 1992, for $50 I purchased a mailing list from an Internet website of all female driver's license holders in the state of Mississippi with the

---

1   In respect for his privacy, I have used this pseudonym for my ex-husband.

birth date of February 17, 1968. I did not purchase lists from other states because of the high cost for me, a single parent. I sent out about fifty letters to names on this list. The only response was from an adoptee who wrote that she prayed I find my daughter.

Many birth mothers and adoptees saw my Internet postings, emailed me and told me about their own search, and asked if I had found my daughter. Through these emails I learned about other sites, and the thousands of others searching for adoptees or birth parents. Many of those birth mothers and adoptees had to use computers at their local public libraries or at their workplaces. This limited access to the Internet left many unable to dedicate the amount of time necessary to do a thorough search. Using information they shared with me by email, I spent many hours searching, and assisted in several matches of adoptees and birth parents. I shared their passion and yearning for reunion.

Most of the birth mothers who emailed me were from Mississippi, and a few had stayed at the King's Daughter's Home in Natchez. Several adoptees lived out of state but were given the information that their birth mother had been a resident of King's Daughter's Home in Natchez. Harkening back to those house rules of 38 years ago, most contacts were by first name only, through email. I never saw the faces of those for whom I completed searches, but I understood what was in their hearts.

Some birth mothers contacted me and shared their stories of belittlement, despair, and feelings of abandonment about their time at King's Daughters. Some of those girls were there the entire time of their "confinement." My time there was not so bad—the house mother was pleasant, and the staff helpful. But I stayed at the home for only six or seven weeks.

In April of 2006, an adoptee named Suzy contacted me and told me she was born in Holly Springs, MS on February 18, 1968. She was looking for her birth mother and asked if I had found my daughter. Her birth date was one day later than what I believed my daughter's birth date to be, and she was born in north Mississippi. I had been told by the

Mississippi Children's Home Society that birth certificates were never altered, so I was certain Suzy could not be my daughter.

I began a search for Suzy's birth mother and we communicated several times. We exchanged photos. When I showed her photo to my husband, he said, "Have you noticed—there's an uncanny resemblance? She looks exactly like you!"

"But she was born a day later and in Holly Springs," I replied.

Suzy had contacted the Mississippi Children's Home Society office in Holly Springs and was told they did not keep records back that far. I told her to contact the main office in Jackson, and that, yes, they do keep records back that far. I knew this was so because I had a letter placed in my file and I had updated my file's information each time I had moved or changed a phone number.

Since I had sought information for others, I knew that the Society required a $250 fee to do a search, so I passed this information on to Suzy. She emailed me later that she had mailed the fee. Both of us shared our hopes that she would find her birth mother.

Several days later I received the call. "Are you sitting down?"

The caseworker said that a young woman had sent in a fee for a search, and that there was a match. She said she had called the young woman, Suzy, and told her my name. She said Suzy's shocked reply was, "We're already emailing each other!"

The caseworker said to me, "Since you are already talking to each other, I can confirm that Suzy is your daughter."

I cannot describe how I felt at that moment to know that after so many years of searching for her face in a crowd, of hoping for a phone call, or a letter, that the face I had been staring into on my computer screen belonged to my daughter.

When I had gone into labor late that night in 1968, and given birth around midnight, I had thought my daughter was born before midnight on February 17. I believed this to be so for over 30 years. I learned from the caseworker's phone call that she was born after midnight. And when I mentioned the birthplace listed on Suzy's birth certificate, the caseworker said perhaps the attorney for the adoptive parents had altered the birthplace. I had no idea this could have been done. And for 38 years I had searched for the wrong birth date.

I remember the morning after my daughter's birth, about 9 or 10 am, the social worker had come into the hospital room with an attorney. They had papers in their hands ready for me to sign. A part of me, deep inside, did not want to take that pen. But I was still a child really, just turned eighteen. I asked the woman, "Am I doing the right thing?" She quickly responded that yes, of course this is the right thing, there was a family just waiting to give my baby the best home and the best of care. I assumed the social worker and the attorney were the authorities, the ones with the answers, and I was young, confused, and trusting. My shaky hand took that pen and signed those papers. At that moment I felt a part of me split off—leaving a powerless self in the middle of an event I thought I had no control over.

When I signed those papers, it was over. That was it. It was too simple. Even at the time, I thought there should have been more conversation, more counseling, and I still believe there should have been something more. But that was it. A human being, a little baby, and her life and mine were changed forever with the movement of a pen.

"Can I see my baby?" I asked a nurse who came in afterwards. She said, "No, not after you've signed those papers. You'll have to ask the social worker."

But the social worker had already gone, and she had taken my baby with her.

I remember later that day when the maids cleaned the hospital room, one asked, "What did you have?" The other said quickly, "She's from 'the Home'." The conversation stopped and I could not say *I don't know*, could not say *I want to see her*.

Later that day, the house mother came to take me back to the Home, and offered, "You had a little girl." I wondered why she told me, but I said nothing. A part of me seemed to have gone away. Perhaps she hoped I would change my mind. At that point, I didn't know I could have. After all, I had signed those papers.

So after thirty-eight years, I was finally about to meet my daughter. Robert and I drove back to the church and waited in the car in the parking lot of The Episcopal Church of the Ascension in Hattiesburg, Mississippi. I had arranged with the rector to meet my daughter there. The rector had left the Parish Hall door unlocked for us. Hattiesburg is a half-way point between Jackson and the New Orleans area, where Suzy lived.

It was a beautiful day, the haze had cleared, and in what seemed like time passing in slow motion I watched each passing car, thinking the next one would be her.

At last, a black Jeep pulled into the parking lot. I could see my daughter as she opened the car door. My heart pounded. Suzy and I, both of us smiling through our tears, walked towards each other in slow motion. Then both of us ran into a long embrace.

After hugging and introductions of our spouses, we went inside the church where Suzy, Phillip, Robert, and I sat at a large table. I could not take my eyes off her. She has the same blonde hair as I did at her age, and curls. The same green eyes. A beautiful smile. She is beautiful. Suzy's husband Phillip remarked on our resemblance, "You two look more like sisters than mother and daughter."

My tears did not want to stop. I wanted to take her in my arms and hold her to make up for 38 years of longing. At the same time, I did not want to overwhelm her.

My husband took many photographs and a few minutes of video, but I did not notice—the surrounding ambiance in the room was as if I was in a dream.

Suzy had brought her baby book, childhood photos, her adoption dress, and other artifacts from her life over the 38 years. She explained the significance of each object she had brought, and I continued looking at her face, her lovely smile. She showed me a photo that her adoptive parents had taken on the day they came to pick up their new daughter at the Mississippi Children's Home Society in Jackson, Mississippi. She was in the cradle that is still used to present babies to their adoptive parents at the Society. The baby lying in that cradle had a mass of dark hair, was two weeks old, and was dressed in white—in the same dress she had brought to show me. I gently cuddled the dress in my arms.

But the most touching thing she brought was a small pink card with the baby footprint taken moments after she was born. Suzy took off her shoe and held up her bare foot to compare the size. "I grew!" she said, and laughed. I reached over and caressed her adult foot for a second, and we all laughed. I held the card with the tiny inked footprint. I looked into that tiny footprint for a long time. I touched it, rubbed my fingers across it. It is the same tiny foot that pressed against my ribs, my soul, my heart. The same little foot that I felt move so many times over those long months, and watched the slow movement underneath my skin. I could almost feel the movement inside again. That tiny footprint had left its mark on my heart, and here it is at last, in flesh and blood and blonde hair and green eyes and the world's most beautiful smile.

I think that even though we both realized that there was a chasm of thirty-eight years between us, seeing each other face to face touched that tiny footprint to both our hearts. And as for me, I could feel my divided self begin to heal.

GHOST IN MY HOUSE
Teresa Martin as told to Jessica Powers

The issues started with Steven. For Steven, there was always a black hole of wanting. He was our oldest, the first of our adopted children to become a teenager, the first who wanted to know about Mom. He would say, "I want my mom, I want to go find my mom."

And we always said, "When you're eighteen, we'll give you all the information we have and you can go find her." We knew then, and we know now, that when he finds her, it'll hurt him. In this case, Mom doesn't want to be found.

One of Steven's brothers was adopted by a gay couple, two men, and they've done everything for this child, giving up their fortune to put him in a residential home during the week. He just can't function in the real world, but he comes home on the weekends. They begged his mother to come participate in therapy with him so he could heal and she just refused.

Another one of Steven's brothers was adopted by his foster mom. They actually did get in touch with his mother but it was for a very short time and it blew up in their face. The foster mom says it was the biggest mistake she ever made.

So I think Steven is in for a big heartbreak. But he really, really wants to know.

It was with Steven when I first realized that the mothers of my children are ghosts, ghosts that live in the same house I do. That other parent is always here, no matter what we do.

Because of the abuse Steven experienced before he came to live

113

with us, he was constantly testing us to see how much we loved him. Every day he was in our house, I had to prove my love to him. Every single day, we started fresh, like there was no past history between us, like I hadn't shown him the day before how important he was to me. Every day was a new day where we needed to show him, once again, how much he mattered. It was exhausting.

His need was so great that we could never recover from one problem before we had to deal with the next. For that reason, Steven is no longer in our lives. He is now living on his own, in another part of the state.

We've adopted eight children through Child Protective Services.

When I think about the future, and how I'll handle it if my other children want to go find their birth mothers, I'm afraid. I don't think I'll handle it very well. Every one of my children is different, and their birth parents are different. For example, I would help Christopher and Elizabeth find their birth mother, Norma. She's a sweetheart. But I wouldn't help them find their father. He would take advantage of them. He's the kind of man who would take money from them. We don't know much about Noah's and Adam's birth mother but, like Trey's and Paul's birth mother, she was prostituting and on drugs and Dad was a pimp. During birth, their mother almost bled out on the table. They had to replace three pints of blood. We don't even know if she's alive now. With that kind of lifestyle, you don't live long.

Most of my children are too young right now to ask a lot of questions about adoption or their birth mothers.

Except Brianna. Brianna, one of Steven's siblings that we also adopted, knows more than the other kids. When my sister-in-law Tabitha was pregnant, Briana started to say things like, "Well, Mommy, when I was in your belly"….and we started talking about how she was never in Mommy's belly but she was in Mommy's heart and we chose her. She wanted to see a picture of the adoption judge and that was all we heard from her. But we would tell her anything she asked.

Adoption is a lot different now than when we grew up, where it was more of a hidden thing in families. Brianna has friends at school who are adopted. It's a very normal thing. I honestly think it would be more difficult for a child growing up in a gay relationship, trying to explain two mommies or two daddies, than it is for an adopted child explaining their situation. That's because there's a widespread acceptance of adoption in society, and many people still don't accept a gay couple raising a child.

Brianna hasn't asked about her mother but she's going to be the first to ask. I will probably tell her that some of her brothers did try to find Mom and Mom didn't want them to find her, that Mom wants to be alone. And I will probably tell her, "It's not because she doesn't love you; it's just that she doesn't know you. You really had no relationship with her, she was busy just trying to survive, and Grandma raised you."

"Before you were a year old," I'll tell her, "you were in my home. You were my child."

I'm not sure Brianna will ever want to know much more. I don't know. We're really the only parents she's ever known. But with Brianna, because of the history of abuse, I will strongly discourage her from getting in touch with her birth mother. I will give her the information but physical contact…? I don't know if that's a good idea. With her father, we can't. There's no way. He was in jail for a very long time. Hopefully, he's still there.

But every child has a question. They all want to know, "Where did I come from?" I think the question they're really asking is, "Who am I?" And they want to know, "Was it because of me that…I mean, did my birth parents just not want me? Was there something wrong with me, is that why they got rid of me?"

That biological link can be very important, but I'm trying very hard to link them to this family through the nurturing part. When one of my kids does something that's characteristic of somebody in the family, I'll say, so that they can hear it, "She's just like you, Mom," or I'll tell them, "That's just like what Grandpa Martin would do." It's not the nature, but the nurturing part, that links them to this family. It's the best I can do. I don't know if it's the right thing or if it'll be enough for them later, but it's all I've got so far.

When my mom tells me about my family history, that's what I look for. How am I like my grandmother that I never knew? And my mom will say, "Your grandmother always hated seeing a child on the street with snot running down their noses. She'd be so proud of you for taking in these kids and caring for them." Hearing about the ways that I'm like my relatives is my connection to my family. That's why I try to make that same connection for my kids with people in the family. But I don't know if that's all they're asking for when they ask that question about their family history.

Also, because we've adopted inter-racially, I'm trying to homogenize cultures. There are arguments on all sides about the right way to handle this, but we're trying to emphasize that they're all American. The boys are just starting to notice their skin color and talk about it. Adam's brown, not black, by the way.

"It's called black, Adam," I'll tell him.

"No, I'm brown," he'll insist.

He'll say, "I'm African-American," and I'll say, "No, you were born in America, so you're not African."

We celebrate Juneteenth and Martin Luther King Day. At the charter school they go to, they prepare for Martin Luther King Day for weeks. And black history, yes, that type of thing is very important to me, as well as introducing them to other cultural things. Like the Jewish faith, we incorporate some elements of that in the home. We celebrate Sedar every year. We celebrate Hanukkah some years. We do it just to bring acceptance and diversity into the home. I think diversity is what I aim for rather than a particular culture, rather than saying to them, "This is what you are." That's true even for my flesh-and-blood children.

For all of my children, I will do what I can to show them that I really care about their history. At the same time, I will gently lead them in the direction that I think is best, and not on a whim. It's not because they come from bad places. It's just complicated. Siblings are no problem. We'll always help them find their siblings. But finding the parents might not be a good thing for them.

It's going to be hard. They're going to feel like whatever I say about their mother is a reflection on them.

I have a lot more compassion for my kids' birth mothers than their birth fathers. In all the cases except one, the fathers have been really non-existent. They haven't even fought for their kids. Christopher and Elizabeth's father fought for them, but he did it because it fulfilled a need in him for power; it had nothing to do with the children.

Sometimes I'm angry at the mothers of my children, for what they allowed to happen or what they did. I'm angry that I'm the one dealing with the consequences of their actions. Other times, when we get a letter from one of them, I feel compassion.

In the end, the birth mother is the important figure for me, for all of my kids. She's the one that's always here, always present in our daily lives.

She's the ghost in my house.

Searching For a Life

Joanne Leeming

I'm really quite drunk. The pub is dark and gloomy; cigarette smoke descends upon us like a swirling mist. A foot away from me, slumped on a velvet covered bench, is a young man: swarthy, slim, good looking, half my age. He's drunk as well. Classic rock blasts from the jukebox. Our feet tap simultaneously, fingers drumming out the beat on solid wood tables. It's like looking into a mirror—we are so alike and yet we only met each other this morning. There is an instant bond between us; a bond of blood.

I don't think my life was ever destined to be a happy one. I seem to have scraped through the last 43 years by the skin of my teeth, avoiding the more harrowing consequences that my behavior should have resulted in and, instead, emerging virtually unscathed, like a cat with nine lives.

One particular event in my life, however, has and will have far reaching consequences and will affect several, if not many, lives for the foreseeable future. I'm talking about the day I naively and selfishly decided at the age of nineteen to become pregnant and have a child without the benefit of a stable relationship, somewhere to live, or an adequate income.

My parents were shocked, yet surprisingly supportive of the pregnancy, especially as Alistair (the father) reassured them that he would marry me. It wasn't long, however, before the relationship failed and I was left alone to face being a single parent. Unsurprisingly the

119

relationship with my parents also failed soon afterwards and I and my bags of carefully amassed baby equipment left home to stay with family friends, Edward and Alice, who cared for single pregnant women until after their babies were born. By this time, I had begun a relationship with Alistair's best friend, Patrick. He was recovering from his own problems, but was a tower of strength and a rock in those unstable waters of 1985.

At first I enjoyed the freedom of leaving home and the independence, but slowly the future became bleaker as Alice interfered more and more with my decisions about the baby. Within a few weeks of moving in with her, she persuaded me to contact the Church of England Adoption Society. "You know you'll never be able to take care of a baby, Joanne," she said, as though she was merely conversing with a friend over afternoon tea.

The more she repeated herself, the more I began to believe her and I allowed one of her church contacts to come and discuss the finer points of adoption. There was something about involving religion, however, that didn't feel quite right and I decided to contact Social Services instead.

After long talks with a very supportive social worker, I changed my mind, as I so often do, telling Alice, much to her displeasure, that I was keeping the baby and that I would cope very well.

On Monday, the 14th of October, I was admitted to Christiana Hartley Maternity Hospital with high blood pressure. When Patrick heard that I was to be induced, he went down on one knee and proposed with the words: "I suppose we'd better get married then!"

The ring was cheap and a larger size than I would eventually need when the swelling in my fingers went down, but I was so happy and couldn't wait to bring my baby into the world. We were going to be a family at last.

Of course for months I'd been petrified of giving birth, and it was probably the most horrific experience I've ever had. The births of my other two children would prove easy by comparison. I spent twelve hours in a pethidine and entonox fueled labor with excruciating backache. At noon the next day, I gave birth to a healthy 8lb 7 oz baby boy with my dark hair and eyes and a red, v-shaped birthmark on his forehead.

Patrick's friend Rob came to visit later that day with his camera and took many photos of us. I look tired, Patrick looks proud, and the baby named Marcus was asleep for most of it. He looked so peaceful.

It wasn't long before sleepless nights, solitude and responsibility began to take its toll and, within days, depression descended like a dark unforgiving cloud. Days merged into night and I felt as though my life had been taken away from me.

"I feel so depressed," I confided to the visiting midwife one morning when I was back in Formby.

She looked at me sharply and replied, "What have you got to be depressed about?"

One week later, I contacted Social Services and asked if I could still have Marcus adopted. In a couple of weeks, I would have nowhere to live because Alice needed my bedroom for her daughter and my parents refused to let me move back in with them. We'd been offered a council flat, but were devastated to find it was on an estate renowned for drug dealers.

In the next few days, I spent time with my social worker, filling in forms describing my appearance, my family and also the appearance and occupation of Marcus's natural father Alistair—who now denied paternity—so that one day Marcus would have some idea of where he came from.

He stayed with Alice until a foster mother could be found and I remember with deep regret the day I walked away from him asleep in Alice's arms. I don't think I even kissed him goodbye. The next day Patrick and I married at the town hall without a reception or a honeymoon.

Within a couple of months, I began to regret my decision, and contacted Social Services to say that I wanted Marcus back. They were extremely obliging and arranged for me to visit him. Contacts took place in a musty, smoke-filled living room where Patrick and I, and his foster mother, Jean, smoked endless cigarettes.

Sometimes we took Marcus out to meet family and friends, slowly beginning to plan a future for the three of us. Unfortunately, although we lived in a more suitable flat, the landlord wouldn't allow children and once again accommodation became a problem.

When Marcus was six months old, depression crept out of the dark corner to which I thought it had retired and, instead of a scheduled visit to see Marcus one sunny afternoon in March, I took comfort in the familiar warmth of my bed.

When Patrick returned home I confessed to changing my mind about keeping Marcus, which infuriated him, as he had been looking forward to being a father. He slammed the door shut on his way out, knocking down our wedding photo, and didn't come back. We remained separated for six long weeks until we eventually reunited and I signed the adoption papers.

Marcus went to an affluent couple who already had a four-year-old adopted daughter and I was reassured that he would keep his name and be told of his adoption from an early age.

I never forgot Marcus, or his birthday, and kept the hospital photos in a secret drawer in my bedroom for the next twenty years. Occasionally, I would get them out and look at them—maybe once or twice a year. But I thought about him every day as I do now. Especially poignant days were his birthday when I would look in local newspapers to see if there were any family announcements that would give me a clue to his whereabouts.

Patrick and I divorced in 1991 after six years and two children, Sara and Joseph. I never told them about Marcus because I was so scared they'd be angry with me for depriving them of a brother. When Sara was fifteen, she confided in me that she had discovered a disused photo album with the words "Me, pregnant with Marcus" written in ink below the empty space where the photo had been. I wasn't annoyed with her, but I was horrified that she had discovered my secret and I tried desperately to explain. I begged her not to tell Joseph and she promised that she wouldn't.

In 2004, the government relaxed the adoption laws and it became possible for birth parents to trace their children. I had already considered putting my name on the adoption register so that Marcus could trace me if he ever felt the need. Unfortunately I never seemed to get around to it because Sara developed her own set of teenage problems and I spent a couple of years concentrating on her and coping with the birth of a grandson. It was only in September 2005 when I was approaching the age of forty and Marcus was nearly twenty that I contacted an agency called "Post Adoption."

It all seemed to go very smoothly. After an initial meeting with Angela, one of the team, I paid £100 towards expenses and naively assumed that we would be reunited within the week. In fact, that didn't happen and although my heart leaped with pure joy to hear that he was still alive, the three letters that Angela wrote to him were ignored and merely antagonized Marcus's adoptive father who made an angry call to the agency.

I was disappointed, naturally, with Marcus's decision not to respond to Angela's letters, but I understood his point of view and resigned myself to the fact that at least I had tried. He now knew I had not forgotten him and maybe in the future he would change his mind about contacting me. At this point in February 2006, Angela asked me to meet up with her one last time to discuss the possible reasons for Marcus's refusal to make contact.

It was in this small, airless room, the scene of several emotional meetings with Angela, that my life changed forever. Maybe she did it on purpose, maybe she was careless, but as Angela spoke, she held the copies of the letters she had sent to Marcus in her left hand and occasionally lowered them so that they were in full view. She did this several times during the course of the meeting and in those few seconds

I managed to read, albeit upside down, words that I was never meant to see: his new surname—Gallant—and a Liverpool postcode.

When Angela and I parted, I looked at her and said, "I'm not as daft as I look."

She appeared puzzled and more so when I indicated the letters that now lay on the table in front of her. Maybe she wasn't entirely innocent of her actions. I'll never know the answer to that question.

For two months I repeatedly trawled the internet, never with any results, searching for clues to Marcus's whereabouts. I became obsessed with his whereabouts, with his appearance, and what he had done with his life. I even considered writing to him to explain my actions. Unfortunately, although my browsing threw up a few clues to his new life—that he'd joined a youth theatre group, and his father was a solicitor—there was no real success.

On Sunday 23rd April 2006 in the early hours of the morning, I typed his name once more into Google. My heart pounded when the first result indicated that a young man called Marcus Gallant, 20, from Liverpool had a MySpace profile. As I clicked on the link, I knew I had found my son. He was so like me that his identity could not be disputed.

I didn't stop to consider my actions and, at three o'clock in the morning, I sent him a short, heartfelt message that included the words, "I'm sorry I gave you away."

At six o'clock, after a restless few hours sleep, I checked my e-mail and was astounded to see that he'd replied.

So here we are, in this bar, two days and many emails later. We are both ecstatic, both amazed that we have been reunited. There are many questions, much laughter and so much talking. We've been talking for seven hours, yet haven't even started. I cannot predict what will happen in the future, but for now, this is all I want. All I need. My happiness is so great that all my problems have faded from view and I am ready to begin a new kind of life.

If I could see into the future, however, I would see that my emotions (and probably his) would become too difficult to cope with. My family life would suffer and my parents would show hardly any interest in their newly found grandson. My daughter Sara would meet him once, but my son, Joseph, would show no interest, and neither would Marcus. Looking further ahead, I would also see that the meetings would become less frequent and any emails reduced from paragraphs to only a few words. I would be forbidden to ever call him or even post mail to his home address. Eventually, the contact would cease completely and the only way I would have any glimpse into his life would be through his MySpace page, on which we would remain silent "friends."

All too soon, I would realize that too much energy was needed to keep the relationship going and that I must patiently wait in the background for many years in the hope that one day he will want to know me again.

Hello and Goodbye
Rhonda Wheeler Baker

Placing my son for adoption was not my first choice upon discovery of my pregnancy. It was the summer before my senior year, and I was only sixteen. I intended to graduate and head off to NYC to become a fashion designer. Pregnancy was NOT part of this plan. I scheduled an abortion, but through a long chain of unpleasant events, it didn't come to pass.

As a pregnant high school senior, I made a deal with God. I would have this baby and give it up, but *only* as long as it was a boy. Boys were foreign to me, and I certainly couldn't raise a boy without a father. So God very kindly agreed that I would give up a son, and that someday I would be the happy mama of a daughter or two. The Catholic priest my mother worked for stepped in and arranged the adoption with a couple he knew in Louisiana. (He had also "arranged" to mess-up the abortion appointment, which I wouldn't find out until years later.) The couple he knew lived next door to his niece, and he'd actually met them, so it wasn't like my baby would be going to complete strangers.

I'd maybe even get news of him now and again.

It was settled.

The birth was dreadful—well, the LABOR was dreadful. I was in awe of the birth, witnessed in the mirror above my spread-eagled body. My body produced a child, and they cleaned him up and handed him to me. I was wheeled out of the delivery room with my black-haired, black-eyed, gorgeous baby boy tucked in one arm, and my teddy bear in the other, the only stand-in for the father that the hospital would allow. I must have looked like such a baby myself.

Back then, moms stayed in the hospital for three days, even after a normal delivery. I intended to make use of every moment to be with my son. Jonathan, my son.

I knew he was not mine—my heart and soul knew that keeping him would be the wrong wrong *wrong* thing to do, and I knew I would not waver. But my son—he was so beautiful—his eyes so dark, promising to be chocolate brown, and thick black hair, olive skin. He was magical, staring so intently about him, never crying, just seeking answers everywhere. He was familiar. I could see my nose, my mouth, my chin in that tiny face. I fell in love, as every new mother is programmed to do. But even as I knew he was not mine, my heart was tearing, shredding. "And a sword shall pierce her heart," says one version of the Bible about Mary's agony. I began to know that agony.

I held him as much as I could, fed him a bottle while my breasts ached to nurse him. There was no such thing as rooming in, and only one designated person could hold him or be in the room while he was there. Had I been a little braver, a little wiser, I'd have broken those rules all over the place. What were they gonna do, take him away?

But I followed the rules, so only my mom and I held him.

If anyone came to visit, I had to bring him back to the nursery. As you can imagine, I hated all visitors, robbers of my time with my baby.

The days passed in a blur. Getting yelled at by Nazi Nurse who found me asleep with Jonathan. Lying alone with a heat lamp between my legs—my episiotomy itched and stung. Getting reprimanded for pushing the help button in the bathroom when I thought I was going to pass out. Wondering over and over again how I could reconcile my longing for my baby and my lack of longing for motherhood. My daddy showing up to visit after ignoring me the entire pregnancy, then crumbling with pride and sorrow in my room. Sitting with my son on my lap as I sobbed and wrote the final pages of a letter to him. A letter that started as a 16-year-old's foolish pen pal meanderings and ended in utter despair, begging forgiveness, praying for understanding. Weeping.

On our last day, we borrowed the priest's 35mm camera and took pictures. They are all taken in natural light, showing a lovely alert baby boy and a sad young girl who is already showing her lifelong mask of grief. The last picture was taken a few moments before 4 pm that day when the circuit clerk would come in with relinquishment papers. At 4 pm, my time was up.

At 3:59 pm, I kissed my son's impossibly soft feet, nuzzled him, inhaling his sweet newborn scent, stroked his hair and put him in his bassinet. Slowly I wheeled him to the nursery, my heart pounding and empty. Marching to a death knell, a nightmare of tile and fluorescent light and sore body and agonizing slow steps. My mom was beside me but I don't remember it.

I just remember feeling terribly, finally, alone.

I knocked on the nursery door, and asked the nurse who answered to please put him right near the window so I could look at him as long as I could.

I pushed him through that door and, as it closed, a wail of pure grief rose from my soul. I cried as a child cries, as a mother cries. The anguish ripped through me, devoured me, and I let it.

I'll never forget the startled faces of the excited new mamas and daddies, their reveries so rudely and bewilderingly interrupted by a distraught teenager.

I turned my eyes to my son as my mother held me up. We wept together.

After a moment, she could not bear it and moved away.

I stood there, my eyes locked on my baby, memorizing his face. At that moment he stirred and for the first time since he was born, I saw him cry. We cried together, my son and I, as if he felt it, too; we were being torn apart, and I was doing the tearing.

At 5 pm, I was still standing there. My mother paced the halls, fuming at the circuit clerk. She would come to stand with me, then pace again.

I was not about to budge. I was taking every second I could get. My eyes did not leave his face. I waited.

Like the condemned wait for death, part of me dying already. I thought I still had time. I could be holding him. I thought, *If I touch him again, I'll never let him go.* I thought, *I will not wreck both our lives. I will wreck only my own.* I realized that all I could do was to stand there, and stare, and weep, and wait.

At something like 6 pm, the clerk showed up. No apologies. By then my tears had stopped, and I was holding the fragile strands of my soul together by sheer will power.

I had to be alone in the room when I signed the papers, so no one could say I was influenced in any way.

My mother hugged me before leaving, whispering, "It's okay if you change your mind…" which only strengthened my resolve.

I signed the damn papers, the word "irrevocable" standing out neon bright. I hated the word, hated that man, hated the people who were taking my baby. Loving my baby, tears scalding my cheeks, barely breathing, I signed the damn papers.

At that moment, I became a new person.

I became a birth mother.

I was wheeled out of the hospital empty handed, empty bellied. I left behind my only child. He would remain there for two more days, until Louisiana law took effect and I signed yet another set of papers that gave him to his new parents. For two days he would belong to no one, have no one.

This thought nearly killed me. I went home to lie in bed and sob. My poor little sisters, so young at the time, did not know what to do.

I slept in my mom's bed, comforted for a few moments at a time before the grief would wash over me anew.

When I found out they named him Tyler, I flew into a rage. Their act of naming him meant he really, really was gone. Grief became my best friend, never leaving my side. The only way to survive was to embrace it.

I never got counseling. I just went back to my life as much as I could. Everything appeared tainted. Nothing seemed worthwhile. Elsa Klensch, a fashion reporter with a show on TV called "Style" made her observation that "Yellow is SO important this season," and I realized that Elsa had no idea what was important. Yellow was certainly not it. Fashion was not it.

The years passed. I studied to become a midwife.

His birthday was the worst: a day to cry, bake a cake, take the day off work, and remember. Mother's Day sucked. I was an unrecognizable mother. I cannot begin to describe the many faces my grief took on. It was my crutch, my shield, my excuse, and, in very bad times, my reason to keep living.

I kept meeting adoptees, dating adoptees. I learned to accept the grim reality that while female adoptees nearly always search for their birth mothers, male adoptees rarely do. I knew that it would be a long wait until I could contact him with any hope of acceptance. I settled in to wait.

I turned thirty in 1996, and that same year my sister had a baby, the first grandchild since my son. At the time I was a live-in nanny and my eyes had been opened to the reality of parenting. These things inspired me to write a letter to Tyler's adoptive mother, thanking her, and asking her very humbly to let me know how he was doing. I knew from the priest and from my attorney that his parents had been reluctant to have any information about me. Despite agreeing to an open adoption, they weren't interested in exchange of information. They seemed very protective and afraid, as if they wanted me to simply not exist. I knew I had to tread carefully, and my letter was a loving and humble request.

I sent it to my attorney, who forwarded it to the adoptive mother's attorney. I waited. I heard nothing.

Later that year, I obtained access to the internet, still a rather new media for the masses. Of course I did an internet search on his name and found it on a role-playing game site.

He was online! He played computer games! He wasn't a baby anymore; he was a kid. A smart kid. He wasn't some stupid drug user like his father, he was a computer boy. The years had suddenly leapt by. There he was. Wow.

I was excited. I was scared. I had information now, an address and phone number that I couldn't do a damn thing with. Nor was I about to. But having that information was powerful. He was alive. He was out there. And someday, when I thought he was ready, I would reach out. Someday.

It was November 28, 2003. I was happily married, had one daughter and another on the way. Thanksgiving was just over. Usually, around the holidays, I did my semi-annual internet search for my son. For eight or nine years, I had found the same thing; old posts he had done on a role-playing game website, nothing more. I had stopped really hoping to find anything new.

This time, I typed in "Tyler Himel," hit enter, and up came something I'd never seen before, a website for poets, and his poetry library. With tons of poems, and a journal by him. His most intimate thoughts and feelings, laid bare and open for the world—for me—to see. I had found my son. I wish I could describe my feelings when I landed on that site, and started reading his poetry. I was exhilarated, terrified, amazed and dazed. I wept.

I read poems about his girlfriend—there were lots of those—and others about the everyday confusing angsty life of a teenager. I read one letter to his dead father; it was touching, poignant and emotional.

Until then, I had no idea that his adoptive father had died. But I looked further, searching for any mention of me, of his adoption. I had to know if he knew, if he cared.

I found it. It was a poem full of anger, directed at a rapist. Right at the heart of the poem was this:

> My mother at fifteen didn't know the names of the
> fifteen that raped her
> But she let me live.
> She bore me for nine months,
> Gave me away in hopes that I had a better chance.
> Gave me away because she couldn't face me herself,
> So now I am faceless.

My heart stopped.

Not only did he know he was adopted, but he thought he was the product of a rape. How utterly horrible.

I sobbed, thinking my poor son believed this about himself.

Who told him such a thing? His parents?

I read on, needing to understand him better. I realized, gratefully, that his anger was not directed at me. I realized that he was intelligent, passionate, knew himself well, and did not break easily. I was relieved. My son was okay. I wrote a poem that night, a response to his beliefs:

Something you need to know

The mother you never knew
Was not raped by one, or five, or fifteen boys
She was young, full of lust and fire
Wet and willing
Just like you
She was a dreamer

A lover
A risk-taker
And thus were you conceived
In a moment of teenage passion
She thought was love
On a pouring-down-rainy night
In the back of her boyfriend's mother's car

The mother you never knew
Made the choice to carry you
Made the choice to give you a better chance
Not because she couldn't face you
But because she knew she was not ready to raise you
Not ready to be a parent

The mother you never knew
Wept
For hours
For days
for years and years
not with regret
but with sorrow
you were beautiful beyond belief
and she let you go

The mother you never knew
Grew up, somehow,
In hazes of grief splintered with
Laughter and inspiration
And made sense of her choices
Made sense of her life

The mother you never knew
Left you alone
To grow, to learn, to be
Left your parents alone
Because she didn't want to intrude

All she knew was that you were alive, nothing more
Until today

The mother you never knew
Is a midwife
Has helped women through birth,
And letting go of their children
Has helped women give birth,
Had her hands on their babies as they
Emerged, wet and sticky
Guided them to their mother's breast
Thought of you
Over and over
Over the years
With each baby
With each Mother's Day
With each March 25

The mother you never knew
Reads your poetry now
In awe of your raw emotion,
Your honesty,
Your passion
And knows exactly where it came from

The mother you never knew
Wants you to know.

I didn't sleep much that night, and went through the next day feeling washed out. I couldn't stop thinking about him, about all that I had learned about him, so suddenly.

It was like a train wreck. I couldn't stop looking. I wanted him to know me. But how?

The website allowed only members to comment on poetry. There was no way to get an email address from it. Even so, I wasn't sure if contacting him was the right thing to do. A battle began inside me. I desperately wanted to contact him, to let him know I was out here. At the same time I was desperately afraid. I felt as isolated and alone as I had the first year after his birth, as if there wasn't a soul who would understand this. I wanted someone to just understand and help me.

My husband Randy was right there, and we talked late into the night.

November 30, from my LiveJournal:

So, after all was said and done, I decided that it felt wrong to me to just lurk around on the poetry site, reading his journals and poetry until I was ready to quit being a chickenshit. My midwife, Pat, who also placed her first child for adoption, has had her son's information for years, and is too frightened to do anything with it. Finally I understand why. When you are a birth mother, you don't know how your child is going to react when you contact them. Will they hate you, because their life was not perfect and rosy? Will they figure since you didn't keep them, you must not care about them, so fuck off? There are a million variables, and every reason to just keep silent.

But it is not my nature to be silent. It is not my nature to hang back. Granted, the past twenty years, and being a midwife, have taught me patience... but there is a time for patience, and I don't feel this is one of those times. There is a reason for everything. He has appeared before me—and now I know more than I ever dreamed of knowing. And maybe that should be good enough. But I don't want to feel like a spy.

So, I am now a member of the poetry website. I have a page. I posted the poem I just wrote the other day, with an author's note apologizing for the shock, and inviting him to come read my LJ, and inviting him to tell me to fuck off if he needs to. Then I went to his poem that referenced his being placed for adoption and commented on it, telling him to please go read my poetry.

Now, all I have to do is wait. My favorite thing. (weak laugh)

A half-hour later, I received an email from my son:

I was not born in portland. Where was I born? Why does your daughter look almost exactly like me? I don't know, I don't know who you are, or your motivation for this. What year was I born? I want proof that YOU are who you say you are before I tell you a damned thing.

My heart pounded and my eyes filled with tears while I laughed with delight! I had been hoping and ready for just such a response. I immediately scanned the photo of me with him, and his parents with him on the day they got him, and sent this message:

I live in Portland now. You were born March 25, 1984 in Kankakee, Illinois—where I was born and raised.

I never met your parents... but this is a photo of me with you just moments before I had to let you go and sign the papers. And this is a photo of your parents the day they got you.

I'm sorry your dad died. I didn't know until I read your poem. My dad died when I was 25.

I don't know what else to say... I want you to be okay with this. If these are not your parents, and I am wrong, I am sorry.

I hit send and waited, breathless. Randy, who I'd been talking with this whole time, waited with me. I was glad for his calm presence.

A long moment later, this reply came:

Yeah..you're right..Alright, I know now, I believe you..What am I supposed to say? What do you want to know about me? Why did you wait so long? How did you find me now?

My response:

Wow. Whew.

You know, Tyler, you're not 'supposed to' say anything. And after 20 years, what do I *not* want to know about you?

Why did I wait so long? You know, from what little I did know of your folks, it did not seem prudent to contact you any sooner.

I wrote you a letter when you were born, that your mom and dad agreed to give you between the ages of 14-18. I also wrote your mom a letter when I turned 30, just letting her know where I was at in my life—but I mailed it to her attorney to give to her. I never heard anything, so I decided I needed to just let it go for a while.

I've had your address and name all your life. I did not want to intrude. And I've talked to dozens of adoptees over the years, both male and female. The men never search. Never. They are not interested in knowing their birth mothers. I—perhaps incorrectly—assumed you would be the same. I figured I would wait until you were 25 or so, until it seemed you might have kids of your own. But then I found your poetry during one of my random searches of your name, and I thought, well, hell. Here he is. And I didn't feel right just lurking around reading your poetry and journal and stuff without you knowing. I'm a very straightforward person and I decided that now was as good a time as any.

Again, I'm sorry if I'm intruding, or freaking you out, or whatever. You are an adult, you have your own life, and it is up to you.

Tyler: *I'm not like any other man you've known. Nobody that gets to know me can say that I am, so maybe that's why I searched. Statistics cannot map out human emotion. I am a college student, I'm 19 now, going to be 20 in march. I'm a print journalism student at Nicholls State University. That's the brunt of my poetry, so you know how I think about a lot of things. I always knew I was adopted, but he wanted me to know you, wanted me to know about the letter. My mother doesn't think I need to know. She thinks that you're going to steal me away from her, and she's overprotective..since my parents got divorced when I was only three or four years old, my dad had no choice but to keep the fact that he knew where you were from me.*

I checked all the agencies I could find in Kankakee about a year ago..I am ready to know..It was my father's dying wish that I knew and now that I do it's an extremely emotional situation for me. I hope that you understand why.

The emails started flying thick and fast now, three or four simultaneous conversations. I read choice bits to Randy, who said, "You are in a lot of trouble—he is a lot like you. He does not communicate provisionally... he's like bam bam bam!"

For two hours we talked that night, through email. We talked about his biological father; the last time I spoke to Teddy, he was on parole. I apologized for not having more info, but Tyler was just happy to know that his birth dad "had a face." We talked about family diseases.

We talked about my family, the circumstances of his birth. There was so much to talk about, so many questions on both sides.

"I am an open book to you," he said. He wanted to meet me. And then he emailed me a picture.

My son is beautiful. He looks like me; he looks like his birth dad.

On December 3rd, we had an emotional conversation that ended with me in tears.

"Goodnight, my only son. Sweet dreams," I wrote.

"Goodnight, mother. Sleep well."

My heart sang.

I could talk about this forever, keep telling all the things we talked about enough to fill up twenty zines. How could I ever describe the joy? My heart is too full. I now have a loving relationship with my son.

For the first time in his life, I was able to give him a Christmas gift, a birthday gift.

We chat online several times a week, we joke and tease, are serious and, sometimes, irritating to each other.

He and Randy, although unrelated by birth, are two peas in a pod. Both geekboys, they have their own conversations. Tyler is forming a relationship with his Aunt Wendy.

We've spoken on the phone a couple of times, and I'll be flying him up here this summer.

I have to laugh at my pathetic attempt to condense this tale into these pages, but there you have it. I will say this. For nearly twenty years, there has been a hole in my soul; a part of me that wasn't complete, as if I was missing just a part of a lung. Every time I thought of him it was an incomplete breath. But now, when I think of him, I can breathe.

My soul is full, my spirit at peace.

My child is with me.

THE LONG ROAD HOME
Chris Weygandt Alba

When I met my firstborn daughter, she stood smoking a cigarette on a sidewalk outside the airport near my hometown.

I hadn't seen her in 21 years, not since she was 24 hours old. I was late, thanks to roadwork, and she was not smiling when I leaped out of the still-rolling car and called her name. I knew her from photographs, as she knew me.

Annika tossed her cigarette and stared at me. I did what instinct demanded, wrapping my arms around her and crying out, "I'd know you anywhere!"

She hugged me back. While we waited for my niece to park the car, we lit up a pair of cigarettes and smiled at each other. *Two peas in a pod*, I thought. *We're going to be okay.*

I was 28 the summer before she was born.

My father's death from cancer had ravaged me, and my marriage to S--- was breaking up. I was a magazine editor in Los Angeles, and I drank hard in nightclubs every evening of the week, dancing as fast as I could to stay ahead of my grief.

I met J--- in a club and loved him immediately because his mother had just died of an aneurism and he understood the loss of a parent. It wasn't much of a reason. But J--- was a funny, smart screenwriter, and he would call me at work and whisper suggestions that made me laugh. I needed to laugh.

My days were like this: Work all day in the copy department of Larry Flynt's *Hustler* magazine. Hit the clubs for happy hour. Fight with my husband, S---. Leave and go to J---'s apartment and drink Bombay martinis. Sleep eventually. Get up and do it all over again.

I went to Cabo San Lucas alone that summer. I walked on the beach and listened to the thundering surf, mourning for my father, drinking in the cabana all day and writing bad poetry at night.

There I had the first inkling that I was pregnant. It came in the form of a poem that flowed through my fingers, unbidden: "O Raoul, the sound of you is round in me..."

I had been unconcerned about birth control with J--- because in seven years of marriage I had not gotten pregnant. I was as undisciplined in that area as I was in all the other areas of my life.

The first thing I did when I returned to L.A. was visit the doctor, who confirmed the pregnancy. The second thing I did was ask for Valium.

The third thing I did was tell J---, and the first thing he did was inform me that we were finished. I was too unstable, he said.

It was 1983. On every radio station Sting and the Police sang their obsessive rant, "Every breath you take, I'll be watching you..." And it was L.A. The movie credits were rolling and cast members disbanding and I couldn't catch my breath.

In a poetic gesture, I smashed the Waterford martini glasses, boxed up the shards, and delivered the gift to J---. I went home and took a handful of Valium, washed them down with gin and waited to die.

After a short stint in a psychiatric hospital, I was able to breathe again, and I made an appointment for a "procedure."

I was still hysterical enough for that nomenclature to strike me as funny. My estranged husband took me to the clinic—more sick laughter. I worked in the most irreverent of industries, and the irreverence was catching.

It was the slimmest of reasons that interrupted the "procedure." The clinic wanted my signature on a form stating that I would remain within a certain distance of the medical facility for the next 24 hours, but I wanted, afterward, to go to my mother's home two hours away.

Because of that, I called a halt to the proceedings. My husband, instead, drove me out to the desert, to my mother, who offered me an alternative. Thus, she changed my life.

Annika exists, in a sense, not because I was heroic but because I wanted my mother. I was a hurt child in the guise of a grown woman. That my recently bereaved mother was hurting as well did not enter my mind.

But she had seen quite enough of death, thank you. As both my father's life and my marriage waned, my mother had tried to rescue us and failed. She was through with things that ended badly. She had a plan.

This plan was simple. She told it to me that night as I sat befuddled and depressed at the dining room table with her and my soon-to-be ex-husband.

"I've talked with the man who has handled our life insurance," she said, holding my hand. "He knows of a family in Southern California that wants to adopt another child. You can have the baby and give it to them in a private adoption. You can even meet them first to see how you feel."

I was fresh out of ideas. I latched onto her idea and clutched it to my chest. It never occurred to me that I could not do it. I just said yes to life.

The decision was a turning point. After meeting the prospective parents and agreeing to a private, open adoption, I quit my job at *Hustler* and went to work on *Los Angeles* city magazine, a healthier atmosphere. I quit drinking and moved back in with my husband, who approved of my mother's plan even if he no longer approved of me.

I worked with a man who was one of J---'s closest friends, and he apprised J--- of my plan. It went over like a lead balloon with him. I soon received brochures about fetal alcohol syndrome. His concern was valid, and I talked about it with my doctor. I alerted the parents to be. We agreed to proceed. They were committed to the baby.

My irreverence didn't vanish overnight: My favorite piece of clothing during my pregnancy was a T-shirt on which I had printed, "YOUR NAME HERE," directly over my burgeoning belly.

I was candid about the coming adoption, and I was frequently told by friends who were themselves parents that I would find it difficult to give up my child.

I didn't argue with them. I did not doubt that I was doing the right thing, and it gave me a sense of peace in what I found to be bizarre circumstances: advancing pregnancy, amiable marital estrangement, clean and sober living, and horrible maternity clothes.

It may have helped that I never had held an infant, nor been close to anyone who went through the process of becoming a mother. It was all virgin territory, and I chugged along like the little engine that could.

One thing was clear to me: I wasn't mother material.

I made it to one Lamaze class. It was an awkward moment because I didn't have a happy husband to coach me, only a good-natured younger brother who was the father of two Cesarean babies. He was interested in natural childbirth. I was not.

I was unprepared for the birthing process. I thought I was getting a case of cramping diarrhea. The pain was shocking, and my younger brother was of little help. So I got an epidural, he got his camera, and we got a nice series of photographs of my mother, me at my evil-looking best, and the birth of my firstborn, a daughter.

Later that night, I was further shocked by a night nurse waking me up to feed "my baby." It was in my chart that the baby was being adopted and that contact between us was to be limited to my initiation of it. But the nurse insisted I feed my little one, as she was busy. She left me with the crying baby and a bottle.

I held the baby awkwardly, both of us squalling, as I vainly tried to get her to nurse from that bottle. It was the worst moment of the entire operation.

Ultimately, I squared my shoulders, took baby and bottle back to the nursery, and presented them to the nurse. She discovered the nipple in the bottle was faulty and, once she had changed the nipple, she offered both baby and bottle back to me. I refused.

I was not mother material.

But I had not yet experienced the truly worst moment. That came the next morning.

My mother arrived. I dressed and packed my overnight case. We walked past a small room where I saw the new adoptive parents bonding with their baby daughter. Something twisted in my chest.

I marched to the parking lot, got in the car, stared straight ahead, that thing twisting inside. My mother pulled up to a red light and stopped. I stared at the light as it blurred, feeling what I could describe only as despair.

The moment ended, and life went on. I had done a fine deed and for the first time felt something like self-esteem.

I had no idea how naïve I was.

The adoptive family was very kind to me. I received numerous photos and keepsakes that year, varying from newborn footprints, a baptismal certificate, to a scrawl on a piece of paper saying, according to the attached note, "I love you, my second mom."

I had asked them to keep in touch, and they accepted a letter from me to my child, to be opened someday when they deemed it fit. I was content.

I settled down and met someone special. With a strange sense of purpose, I told him I wasn't using birth control, and he agreed. Within a year, I was pregnant again.

The day the home pregnancy test showed positive, I drove to work with an ancient song in my heart: *Blessed am I among women!*

This time, I was mother material.

My second daughter, Milo, was born 20 months after Annika. I was captivated by her. I lived apart from her father and became a single mom, got a better job, bought a home.

Now, when the photos and newsy letters came from Annika's mom, I felt pain. Annika looked uncannily like me. I sent newsy letters in return, but I began to understand what I had given up, and the fierce maternal feelings were bittersweet.

The reality of the gift I had given to Annika's parents was demonstrated daily in my own daughter, and so I learned to live with a sense of sorrow mixed with pride. When the subject of children came up in conversation, I said I had two, but one was adopted out. As the years went by, I had a number of wonderful talks with adoptees who expressed joy at meeting a birth mother willing to talk about her experience. I found comfort in the idea that I could "represent" birth mothers in those exchanges.

I did a little research on the Internet and learned that guilt and grief are common emotional repercussions of giving up a child. Grief, I felt, but guilt? I gave my firstborn to a wonderful family. I didn't feel guilt about that.

The sense of loss never waned, and apparently, that's common. If a 1989 study in Maine is indicative of reality, *every* birth parent wants to be found by the child who was relinquished, and 95 percent of adoptees would like to be found by their birth parents.

One day in late January 2002, I opened a letter from Annika's mother, who had not written in a number of years, since shortly after the family had moved to the Midwest.

"I have a feeling it will not be long before Annika contacts you," she wrote. "I know a lot of thoughts are on her mind."

There followed a long description of Annika, who had finished high school and was almost 18. She was a good but troubled child. She was smart, rebellious, searching for something her parents couldn't provide.

"I hope and pray that God will lead her in the right direction," her mother wrote. "She seems at times to have very low self-esteem. Please keep her in your prayers, as she is trying to discover herself…."

In my imagination, Annika was happy, strong, and headed for college. I was frightened by this letter. I felt responsible for her low self-esteem. I wondered if the adoption had scarred her for life. I considered for the first time that maybe my genetic make-up would make her life miserable.

Then came Annika's own letter, slightly shy, a little cool, and full of information about herself. She said she had questions but she asked none. She spoke of fighting depression, and of moving out on her own. She referred to the decision to "put me up for adoption," which made me cringe.

Her parents, she wrote, "have made it very clear to me that you made your decision out of love and consideration for me so I have no feelings of remorse or hatred towards you."

I responded immediately and joyously: "For 18 years," I told her, "I've hoped that one day I would be able to tell you how precious you are to me."

I tried to clear up the notion that she had ever been "up for adoption." "I learned about your parents right after I learned about you," I told her, "and you were claimed and wanted before you ever took a breath." It seemed important to me, that distinction.

For three years the letters flowed, divulging information and feelings, discussing the difficult issues surrounding her adoption. Each letter was a risk, both of us wondering just how safe this all was.

My research into adoption had hinted that she and I were deciphering what we did or didn't do that led to the situation.

For me, Annika's adoption was a gesture of love for her, but also a failure on my part to provide a good home for her. For her part, Annika openly wondered why I had "given her away," a natural question stemming from the sense of rejection experts say an adopted child feels at some point in growing up.

But there was joy in the process of discovering "why I am the way I am." In appearance and temperament, Annika bears a strong resemblance to me, and uncovering the similarities gave us both a feeling of belonging.

We had our reunion on Annika's 21st birthday, three years after her first letter. It was a rocky start at the airport that day, my being late for our first meeting. We stood around for several minutes, studying each other, smoking our cigarettes, and noting commonalities. We made small talk.

The first thing we did was visit the California Central Coastal ocean, a rocky beach midway between L.A. and San Francisco, where I now lived. She hadn't see the beach in the years since her family moved to the Midwest, and she was happy there. We took long walks on the beaches around my country, sometimes with my husband, sometimes just the two of us. It was a long, slow building of a relationship over an emotional distance.

At my home, we talked at length, and I showed her the scrapbook I have kept of her life. I showed her family photos of her long-dead ancestors. She stayed four days.

The extended family gathered, made up of cousins, aunts, uncles, grandma and great-aunt, and they welcomed Annika to the family. The only person she didn't get to meet was her half-sister Milo, who was working in Los Angeles.

We spent days talking about our likes and dislikes, our histories, our parents. She found her roots, and I found my first-born daughter. "This is the most profound thing that has ever happened in my life," she told me.

The years passed with letters and phone calls between us. Annika went through a few years of turbulence, and she left the home of her parents and struck out on her own in the Midwest. I received long, heart-rending, soul-searching letters. I chose to advise her as a mother would, although she had one of those already. Annika didn't mind, apparently, that I claimed a motherly role in her life. "You're different from my mom," she told me. "I can tell you anything, and you don't freak out."

I didn't freak out because I had a clear sense that another mother raised her, and Annika was somehow my child on borrowed time.

Three years after her first visit to my home, Annika came back again for Christmas, and we shared some of our different holiday traditions. She cooked aebleskivers for me, as she learned them from her Danish mother, and I stuffed a stocking for her on Christmas Eve. Christmas gifts were a strange issue. Nearly everything I purchased for her was not quite right. They were returned to stores and exchanged for something else. But she fell in love with some things of my own and was thrilled when I gave them to her. Go figure.

Our contact over the past seven years grows stronger and feels more securely loving. We email, we write letters, we talk on the phone, and we have camped together with family at a state park halfway between our homes. Annika has left home in the Midwest to make a life for herself in Portland. She's working and going to school. We talk excitedly about her future as the birth daughter of what she calls a "strong mother."

Ours is not exactly a mother-daughter relationship, but it has the earmarks of one. I have not usurped the position of her mother in her life, but I treat her like a daughter. She calls me "Bio Mom."

She sent me a birthday card this year that says it all for me:

Chris,

You're one of the most amazing people I've ever met. A day doesn't go by that I'm not grateful for the sacrifices you made for me. I love you more than words could ever say. Thank you for being the beautiful being that you are.

Love, Annika

Annika is her own person, and we are not "two peas in a pod," as I first imagined we were. Getting to know her has helped me let go of my feelings of guilt and my visions of how things ought to be, because she is most definitely her own young woman. Through both my daughters I have learned to love without conditions, accepting their differences, the sometimes prickly relationship they are trying to forge. I'm not a perfect mother to either of my two daughters.

Annika and I have found a unique partnership. We go to poetry readings in our two separate cities and compare experiences, encouraging each other to explore our poetic voices. We have written poetry together, by alternating lines. In one we called "The Border Between Us" we tried to put into words the substance of our reunion:

> We steer down the winding road,
> past the fences and the shadows,
> where young oaks struggle to rise under old oaks
> and we describe ourselves
> mother, daughter, separated at birth,
> going through the motions
> that enlighten the hearts of two
> who were destined from their beginning
> to find each other.

CLOSING IN FOR THE PICTURE
Amanda Angel

I stood in the hotel parking lot, examining every car that pulled in, hoping to see a little girl sitting in the back seat. My stomach spiraled and swirled, imitating the curly ribbon on the gifts I held. Did we have the plans correct? Was I meeting them here or at the restaurant? My thoughts twirled, wondering if this meeting would go well or be filled with too much emotion. After all, this meeting up with my birth daughter Meg and her parents, Anne and Will, would be the first time after about five and a half years. The plan was to connect during their ski vacation with friends, just days before Meg's seventh birthday.

Because I'd been unsure of how comfortable our meeting would be—for Meg, for her family, and for me—I had made plans to stay at a different hotel than the family. I knew I would need a place to process everything on my own and I was pretty sure they would need their time away from me too. Waiting for that whole visit to begin was a bit like preparing for an awkward first date, and even that thought sent my stomach looping around again. I found myself mentally rolling over potential conversation starters; my palms grew sweaty just thinking about the meeting and, as I waited, my breath became a little staccato.

Then Meg's parents drove into my hotel's parking lot, the car slowed and Anne hopped out of the front seat. As Will came around the back of the car to give me a hug, Anne opened the back door. There Meg sat with a huge grin on her face. The grin grew even bigger as she focused in on the gifts I had in my arms.

"Are those for me?" she asked.

Anne unbuckled Meg from her booster seat and she flew out of it, racing toward me.

Time moved in slow motion as I took in her lengthy legs, crystal violet eyes, long brown hair—all moving towards me. Her outstretched arms wrapped around my legs.

After that initial burst of excitement, she quickly retreated, dropping her arms at her side, suddenly shy. Did she feel like she was stepping over boundaries? Why had she suddenly gone shy?

She looked me right in the eye and with a quiet, "Hi, Amanda," she moved back to the car and hopped in. I got into the backseat and sat next to her. How strange to be sitting next to my own daughter, a stranger.

Meg and I both proved skittishly nervous about how to interact with one another, although her parents seemed calm about the whole thing. Meg filled our discomfort by talking a lot, telling me that she knew we both shared February birthdays, how she thought being a Valentine baby was really neat, that her birthday was only a few days away, how she had remembered that I was adopted too. She asked if I ever met my birth mom like she was meeting hers. What did I like to do? Who else was in my family? Without taking a breath, she moved from topic to topic: her bedroom décor, what she liked about school, words she knew in Spanish, her best friends, her boyfriends (yikes!). I recall realizing that endless chatter is sometimes the way I deal with nerves too.

Seeing her, now a young girl as opposed to the baby she had been the last time I'd had a visit with her, caught me a little off guard. She had her birth father's eyes, which triggered memories of him. Her hair was damp and tangled from swimming at the hotel pool. She was dressed casually after a day of skiing. I knew, though, that she loved to don a fancy dress here and there. She seemed to love the sweater and corduroys I had brought her for her birthday. I could smell chlorine and sweat with the thank you hug we shared. It was the smell of an active kid.

It's funny. Physically, I didn't see myself in her as much as I saw her birth father, so sometimes it seemed unbelievable that she had 50 percent of me in her genes too. But then I noticed the way she tilted her head and smiled. That was me. The way she rubbed her hands together? I've always done that. Her chattiness turned out to be only one of the many similarities we had. But Anne was a talker too. That was one of the things that drew me to her as an adoptive parent. Had Meg developed the traits I was witnessing via nature or nurture? Were they innate or learned?

While I was with Meg and her family, my head that evening filled with spinning thoughts and observations, and our interactions contained at least a few uncomfortable silences. Although happy to see her again, I was thankful that it was a relatively short visit. When the subject of this visit was first broached by Anne, I had been hesitant. Was I ready to face questions or even judgment? Will and Anne had been so excited for me to meet with Meg, as well as their close family friends; it was as if their family pride embraced me too. We had made plans to meet alone for a bit and then their friends would join us for dinner. That had been fine with me; I figured it was a smart idea to have their friends along to provide a buffer when things got awkward. But fortunately, things didn't get awkward. In fact, I was surprised at how open and welcoming they all were.

As we dug into our meals, Meg sat across the table from me and studied me with quick but precise glances. I think the kids around her were a welcome distraction when she would become uncomfortable. She could look away and go back to coloring placemats or being silly with the others. Over the time we ate, she warmed up enough to sit on my lap.

It was strange to feel her weight there. The last time she had sat in my lap, she was 14 months old and easily cocooned in my arms. Now, she was tall and strong yet still open to my embrace. I wondered how it was so easy for her to accept me. I could feel that she really loved me even though I had only been on the periphery of her daily life. "This feels nice," Meg said.

I couldn't have agreed more. "Yeah, it does, Meg."

The next morning my pajama-clad daughter showed up at breakfast, "Good morning, Manda. I want to sit on your lap," and immediately crawled into my lap.

I watched Anne and Will for any signs of discomfort or defensiveness. Instead, I was met with smiles and hugs.

With an ease that surprised me, my arms moved to wrap around my little girl.

She tucked her arm around my neck and sweetly whispered, "I'm really glad that you're my birth mom. I love you." She nuzzled her angelic face into the crook of my neck as she had as a newborn.

Phew. I wasn't ready for the emotions her tenderness evoked but I held it together through breakfast.

Anne suggested that after breakfast we head up to their hotel room to watch some home videos they had brought along. And so I found myself sitting on the hotel bed, Meg spread across my legs, as we watched scenes of Meg trying out her dramatic skills onstage during a school performance of The Velveteen Rabbit, then scenes of her dancing hip hop and presenting a power point she had made for fun.

It was touching that they thought to bring these recorded memories to share with me. They portrayed moments that can't be captured in just words or pictures bundled into a mailing envelope. They demonstrated that some of Meg's flair for performance came from my love and involvement in theatre. It was an unexpected gift to peer even deeper into this family's life and to know even more about Meg.

Hugging each other and saying goodbyes, Meg hopped up on the unmade bed and asked one final question. "Amanda, will you adopt again?"

I stared at her, unsure of what she meant.

Anne jumped in to the rescue, "Meg, do you mean will she ever place a baby for adoption again?"

"Oh. Yeah. That's what I meant, Mom."

I hoped not. Saying that would imply that it was bad or wrong. But I did hope to have more children someday that I could raise with a husband. My head reeled with the knowledge that my heart couldn't handle placing another child for adoption, especially when all I've ever wanted was to be a mother. "No, Meg," I finally responded. "Why do you ask?"

Taking a deep breath and swirling the white sheets with her feet, Meg said, "I want to be the only one."

Melt. I felt heat rise up my throat and spread across my face. My voice was shaky, holding back tears. "Oh, Meg, you'll always be my only first born. I'll always love you. You're so special to me."

She quietly slid off the bed and came over for one last hug. "Come visit me. Okay, Amanda?"

"I'll try."

I smiled and waved as I walked out of their hotel room. I held it together until the minute I steered my car onto the freeway for the three hour trip home. Then, speeding down the freeway, tears streamed down my face. I don't think I had cried that hard since the day I handed her to her parents, seven years prior.

Back at home, the entire evening following the visit I could hardly control body-heaving sobs while I paged through her baby books and reminisced, telling my parents about the visit. My mom sat on the couch and held me. She told me that she was proud of me and I had made the right decision to meet up with Meg.

My dad hugged me and said, "I'm really proud of you, kiddo. You did a really tough thing and everyone made it through just fine."

In retrospect, it was a wonderfully nerve-racking and loving meeting. This opportunity provided Meg with more knowledge of who I was; it gave me a chance to see and know how happy she was and how she and her parents had an incredible relationship.

I think Meg's parents came away from this meeting feeling as though we did the right thing, opening our worlds a teensy bit more than before to one another. It was especially good for Meg because it gave her more information and connection about herself. At the time, I think I knew that it was helpful to meet on neutral territory; we weren't venturing into either of our homes or even realities. Somehow, it helped to maintain that quiet separation that is a natural consequence of adoption.

Eight months later, Anne contacted me, saying Meg had asked to see me again. After Anne suggested visiting Meg at their home, I vacillated over how it would affect Meg both emotionally and mentally. Would she understand, at the age of 7, what was truly happening? Would she be able to handle the balance of mom and birth mom in her own house, her safe zone?

This was opening up an entirely new chapter. Would her parents treat me differently when I was on their "turf"?

Would being in their home be uncomfortable for everyone involved? What would other people think about this arrangement? Would my parents think this was a good step for me to make? After all, this was new territory for me, as both a birth mother and an adoptee.

My siblings and I did not grow up knowing our birth parents. Just as I think many adoptees do, I had created a fairy tale idea of what my birth mother would be like. I dreamed up entire story lines of what she had said to me when I was born or how she would smile at me if she ever met me. I imagined the tight hug she would give me or the way she would look up while retelling her stories about being pregnant with me. But I was having her answer questions the way I wanted her to answer them. This is the mirage we adoptees create—a story that isn't really there. What if Meg's fairy tale mirage of me was destroyed with my arrival? What if spending over 24 hours changed her fairy tale ideas of me?

And in a moment of honest self-preservation, I wondered, Could I handle it? What if I would walk in and feel an overwhelming sense of grief? What if I started crying in front of them? What if I wasn't strong for her? What if I scared her by launching into a repeat of my personal sob fest during my drive home months earlier?

The ski vacation had been hard enough to process and that was only dinner and breakfast together. What would happen when I was staying for two nights under their roof? I brought my thoughts back to Meg. What if spending a weekend together under the same roof would send her into years of therapy? What if she thought I was weird or boring? What if she didn't like me? Should I hug her? Could I hug her?

But finally, I realized that, because her family suggested it, they must be comfortable with the idea of me visiting. So, I purposefully set aside my neuroses and agreed.

Recognizing Meg's house from pictures, I pulled into the driveway. I cut the car engine. My heart pounded hard against my ribs. Cold light beamed through the overcast day, through the windshield, hitting my white-knuckled hands gripping the steering wheel. This was it. Shadowy movement in the house caught my eye. My stomach rolled. I ruffled my fingers through my ponytail in a nervous attempt to calm myself. Why was this so hard? It's not as though it was the first time I was meeting my daughter. After all, I had just seen her months before. Anne and Will sent pictures at least once a year. With each packet, I watched Meg grow and change from afar. They always shared each of her milestones. When Meg climbed up on the counters to get chocolate, her mom sent a report. When Meg learned to crawl, Anne sent a photo of her crawling toward some live lobsters. I witnessed her childhood stories through the voices of her adoptive mom and dad. When Meg learned to talk, they wrote about how she called me "birma" when they would talk about me. So I wasn't a complete stranger to her. After our earlier visit, she had seemed content in the reality that she had two moms and a dad in her life right now.

So, here I was, 29 years old, feeling as anxious as I had for the first day of school. Anticipation. Nerves. Excitement. All of the emotions were present. As I uncurled my knuckles from the steering wheel, they regained their color. I coached myself as I looked down at my hands. *Think positively. You are not an imposition on their reality if they've invited you.* I pulled the keys from the ignition, took a deep breath, and opened the car door slowly, telling myself, *It will be new and different, but good for all involved. Right?* Walking as though I had more confidence than I felt, I approached the front door.

Before I could even reach out to push in the doorbell, Meg threw the door open and smiled her toothy grin. I saw that an adult tooth was coming in and her eyes were an amazing purple, even more so than I recalled. She had changed so much, even in eight months' time.

It was still shocking, even after our last visit and years of receiving pictures, to see how much she resembled her birth father. It always caught me off guard. In that first instant, I caught my breath and my mouth momentarily felt paralyzed.

I blinked out of the moment of recognition and stood there, flashing a closed-mouth smile. I raised my hand, giving a small wave to acknowledge her as she peeled herself away from the door, yelling, "Mom! Mom! She's here! She's finally here!"

Anne appeared with a vacuum, its cord tangled in her hand. She dropped it with a loud thud and smiled.

Secretly, I reveled in the fact that she was concerned about the state of their house, as though she was trying to show me that they provided everything they promised. Dust or no dust, I still knew that she and her husband were the "right" parents for Meg.

She threw her arms around me, welcoming me into their home. A home filled with pictures of our daughter, her artwork, and the feeling of a family. It was a perfect match to what I had predicted and hoped for. Clean, sophisticated and homey.

I was quiet, taking everything in.

Meg was pulling and swinging Anne's arm as we stood there.

I immediately noticed how happy they were, how real their interactions with were each other. "Meggie, run upstairs and grab Tigger. Amanda would probably love to meet him."

Meg bounded up the stairs, "Okay, Mom. Amanda, you'll really like him! He's really cute. I'll be back."

Anne and Meg were just like any other mom and daughter combination. Why this was surprising to me, an adopted child myself, is odd. I have a terrific relationship with my parents, so why had I thought it would be any different?

Then I was given a tour of the house and couldn't help but think that I could have never provided this life for Meg.

It was comfortable in their home, with this family. It seemed they carried on as though this was a typical day. I was not influencing how they spoke to one another or how they loved one another. It was good to see how content Meg was in her own home. She was just being herself. I liked that I knew that. I liked feeling her ease and knowing that she was confident here with her parents.

It made me miss the opportunity to experience this life with her. Being the one to prepare her for school, make blueberry pancakes together, read before bedtime. I was her birth mother but never did any of these things after she was a month old. That was when she was carried into this new world.

Standing in her world, I was in the midst of an experience that was completely out of my control. This time, I couldn't dictate how I might react, retreat to my own hotel if it got awkward, or stop the barrage of what ifs that pummeled me.

After exchanging pleasantries about my trip up north to their house, I escaped to retrieve my overnight bag and to give my nerves a chance to settle. That's hard to do when your brain is whirring like a baseball card stuck in a bike wheel. *Thlip, thlip, thlip.* Why was I always so nervous at these meetings? This child was not a stranger. She's my flesh and blood; yet, this meeting felt awkward to me. It was as though we were all silently watching, analyzing, thinking, judging, trying not to judge.

While rummaging through my car, I made a choice not to overthink or judge and to face my fear. I slammed the car door and slung my bag over my shoulder then walked around my car. A little trail of fairy figurines peeking out of the garden caught my eye. I had heard about this garden of Meg's. So creative! I smiled and wondered if she had gotten that imaginative spark from me or if it was something her parents cultivated. Perhaps it was neither. Maybe that was just Meg. No other influence, but that of her own imagination.

Slipping back into the front foyer, I asked Anne where to put my things.

She smiled and just looked at me. What might she be thinking? Was she as nervous as I was to open up her home to her daughter's birth mother? Unlocking their life for me to step in couldn't be easy. After a moment, she showed me the guest room I could use but not before mentioning that Meg wanted to have a slumber party in her room. With me. All alone.

Oh my....

I didn't know how comfortable I was with this idea, especially because I was afraid Meg would want to ask questions that I wasn't ready to answer. However, Meg rocketed down the stairs, kitten in hand. "This is Tigger. Isn't he cute? Amanda, do you want to have a slumber party with me in my room tonight?"

I looked at her and shoved my "No thanks" response back down inside. How do I say no to this sweet little girl who happens to be my daughter?

She must have noticed my hesitation and simply said, "Or you can sleep in my bed and I can sleep with my mom and dad if you want or I can have a slumber party in my room with you."

I asked her what she wanted and she said, "You."

I felt my heart heave a bit at that loaded answer. In that moment, that one word made me question every decision I had ever made regarding Meg. She had no way of knowing her response sent me spiraling, but it did.

Anne's hands rested gently on my shoulders and, with a reassuring squeeze, she asked Meg to grab my things and take them up to her room while we started dinner in the kitchen.

Anne fixed me a glass of ice water and I sat at their breakfast bar. "So, Amanda, you're back in school to become a teacher? How do you like it? I loved teaching. I miss it sometimes."

I was amazed at the ease of our conversation, like two girlfriends just chatting about their lives. Our talk moved from topic to topic. She laughed as she told me a story about how all of her close friends thought it was so strange to invite me to visit and stay in their home.

Anne couldn't believe how ruffled and confused her friends got, but I could. It was even a little strange for me. How were Anne and Will so comfortable letting me in? In my own family, most of the four of us didn't know our birth parents. Even now, as adults, only one sister has opened her adoption. However, this entire family was excited about sharing our time together.

Still, had I been one of Anne's friends, I would've questioned allowing me—this woman, this birth mother, essentially a stranger—into her life.

During this visit, we headed out to Meg's softball game. Crossing the field, I again grew nervous. Now we were in public. What if people had questions? How open were Anne and Will with all of their friends about Meg's relationship with her birth mother? We walked toward the diamond and Meg yelled out to her teammates, at the top of her lungs, mind you, "This is my birth mom! She's here! My birth mom is here."

Wow. That wasn't awkward at all.

Some parents turned to see the commotion and then went back to conversations; a few stared a tad too long for my comfort. What did they think about me?

The game started and I settled on a patch of grass next to a friend of Anne's. We talked about how I was Meg's birth mom and she thought it was really neat that we were in contact. During a break, Meg came and plopped herself down in my lap. I wasn't used to her being this close to me. Being a birth mother wasn't something that I lived out every day. It was new, foreign, and in public. I couldn't escape the idea that people were silently judging me. How strange would they find this? How would Anne react to Meg being so affectionate and comfortable with me? I did a quick scan; no one seemed to care. I probably thought more of it than any of them did.

Then… Anne's friend leaned over with a smile and casually asked, "So, was it a one night stand?"

Seriously? Seriously. SERIOUSLY! Who does that?!?

Caught off guard, my face burned red. I was offended by the insinuation and bumbled over my response, saying, "No. It was a relationship of a couple years that I had thought would end in marriage." I explained there were just some major glitches that ended the relationship and led to the decision to give Meg a better opportunity for the life she deserved. But I knew I shouldn't have to defend my morals or who I was for making such a difficult decision. The insinuation felt like a punch in the stomach, just as I had been getting comfortable enough to publicly wear the title of birth mother.

Plain and simple, birth mothers are subjected to stereotyping. It may not always be vocalized but it's often there. And we all fear it. The revelation of our roles as birth mothers, that we placed a child for adoption, is so scary. We worry, *What will people think?* Whether it's the belief that we were teenagers who didn't know better, addicts who couldn't take care of a kid, whores, uneducated, poor, bitter, vengeful, maybe even on the hunt to take our children back—all of these assumptions hurt. The realization that people will jump to any negative conclusions before positive ones, that they decide what we did was unimaginable without hearing our stories, cuts deep. I am none of these stereotypes and most of the other birth mothers I have met aren't either.

I was simply a young woman who couldn't be a parent at a time when I found myself suddenly about to become a parent. I couldn't provide her with a life that would have been comparable to what she has now. Her birth father and I were at odds and no child deserves to be put in the middle of that kind of situation. I wanted to do what was best for the daughter to whom I gave birth.

Rather than dwell on the question of this stereotype, it filled me with pride to know that Anne and her husband, Will, recognized the good about me. They didn't pass judgment. They never questioned what type of a person I was. They trusted me. They loved me.

After the game and as the night moved on, Will came home for dinner. He welcomed me with a smile and a hug too. His pride in Meg poured out of him as he shared many of her successes, in and out of school. The conversation carried on over dinner, with Meg behaving as though she was thoroughly embarrassed but secretly pleased by her dad's praise. Instead of being bored by the adult conversation, Meg joined in. She was comfortable to take such an active part. It was a different side of her than I had seen during our last visit. She seemed less restrained.

Meg helped her mom carry dishes into the kitchen, while Will and I spoke about his newest passion, teaching college courses.

Upon her return to the table, Meg suggested that we get pumpkins to carve for Halloween. On the ride over to the pumpkin patch, Meg and Anne pointed out the local areas they frequented.

I asked Meg to share how her year in school was going so far.

She said she had a lot of friends from all different groups. I wondered if she felt as though she didn't fit anywhere specific or if she was the person who created binding between many groups. Her maturity surprised me. She was so conscientious of other people and how her actions affected them. In that short ride, I couldn't help but smile. How lucky I was that my daughter, with the guidance of her amazing parents, was simply incredible.

Our pumpkins had been picked just as rain started to fall. Fat droplets spattered on our faces, enjoyable refreshment. Splashing in quickly forming puddles, we ran to the car.

As a treat, Anne suggested heading to one of their favorite restaurants for a slice of pie.

Sitting in the booth across from Meg, I finally had the chance to study her features more closely. As she chatted with her mom about a friend of hers at school, I stared. I moved past her eyes, which mirrored her birth father's shape and size, to really look at her.

What a beauty. Classic. Natural. Unaware of it. Mountains of whipped cream on top of her slice of pie caused Meg to widen her eyes, and then she asked me to tell about her birth and some information about her birth father.

Here we go! I thought. *The point of no return.* I had expected this conversation as I had the same questions about my own birth. I just hadn't expected Meg to ask so soon.

I wasn't sure how much detail I wanted to share about her birth. It was something I held private. I skipped a lot of information regarding my relationship with her birth father. I explained that I loved her birth father and we almost married. We both wanted what was best for her. But I also saw that she was still too young to understand the particulars of our partnership that had led to its ultimate demise. And it wasn't my place, at this point, to cloud her ideas and expectations of him. It would be up to her if she wanted to pursue a relationship with him.

Rather, I told her about her birth—that we had gotten stuck in the snow on the way to the hospital, that my labor with her was fast, that she was beautiful despite two little bumps on her head from the moment her head crowned, that I loved her even more once I held her in my arms, and that she lived with me and my family until it was time to go to her adoptive parents.

It was hard to give her the details of her birth and the time I spent with her in my home. There were some personal moments that even now I usually keep to myself. They are ways for me to connect to that point in time, when I was her mother. How do you explain what it was like to get up and feed her in the middle of the night and then clean up after she sprayed formula through her nose like a scene from a horror movie? I was the one who got to rock her while singing my favorite lullabies to her. The month I had with her from birth to placement had been my time with her—being her only mom.

As she grows older, I envision more questions, tougher questions coming my way. For now, I felt good about the conversation we had, especially because she seemed so content with her new information.

On the ride back to their house, rain hit the windshield hard, providing noise where there was otherwise silence. The conversation had died down to be replaced by thoughtful musing. It was a sign to me that we were all okay with one another.

Pulling into the garage, Meg squealed that it was time to carve the pumpkins. We lugged them into the kitchen, laid down newspaper and started cutting off the tops. One of my favorite parts of carving pumpkins is pulling the mushy guts out. So, pulling my pumpkin lid off, I dove into the stringy mess inside.

Meg stared with awe and a smile crept across her face. "Do you like doing that? My mom doesn't. But you do. I must have gotten that from you."

Now, I don't know that genetics really dictates one's love for pumpkin goo, but I felt honored that she made that connection. It made me feel like I was her mom instead of a guest or visitor of hers.

Anne pulled out pans for seeds and let me and Meg share our time on the floor, cutting out pumpkins. She worked in the kitchen, chiming in here and there, but she seemed to want to stay in the background, letting us share this experience as we finished our masterpieces. To mark the artistry of our carvings, we lit them and posed next to them while Anne joked and smiled and took our pictures. I loved that Meg snuck in close for the last picture. It helped me to know for sure it was all okay. Okay enough that I felt I could have that slumber party and I knew how lucky I was and still am.

CONTRIBUTOR BIOS

CHRIS WEYGANDT ALBA is a journalist living on the central coast of California. A former editor on the staff of several magazines, she now writes essays and interviews for a small community publication. She's an award-winning gardener and writer of ultra-short fiction as well as a poet. She met her first born daughter, who had been given up at birth, a few years ago when her daughter was 21.

AMANDA ANGEL is an elementary school teacher in Milwaukee, Wisconsin. In 2000, she placed her daughter in an open adoption. Since then, she has become an advocate for both birth mothers and adoption. Although she has written plays including *Three Rocking Pigs*, a children's musical produced for Marquette University, this is Amanda's first book.

ANN ANGEL is a professor of writing at Mount Mary College in Milwaukee, Wisconsin. The editor of *Such a Pretty Face: Short Stories about Beauty* (Abrams/Amulet 2007), she is also the author of several biographies for teenagers, including the forthcoming *Janis Joplin, Rise Up Singing* (Abrams/Amulet 2010). Ann is the adoptive mother of four children, including her daughter Amanda, with whom she edited this collection. Please visit her website at www.annangelwriter.com.

RHONDA BAKER met her son and his parents just before her fortieth birthday. It was every bit as terrifying as she ever imagined it would be—and every bit as wonderful. She is nearing completion of her first novel, and she and her husband are working on an adventure series for middle readers. She lives in Portland, Oregon, with her husband and daughters.

MAUREEN CIGANEK is an adoptive mother and art teacher whose passions include reading and writing. She holds a bachelor's degree in art education, a master's degree in art history, and has studied creative writing at Mount Mary College in Milwaukee and at the Iowa Summer Writing Festival, University of Iowa, in Iowa City. She lives with her husband and son in Milwaukee, Wisconsin.

PATTI CLEARY, a writer, editor, and publisher, lives near the ocean in the mid-atlantic region of the east coast with her husband Michael and their menagerie of twelve rescued cats. She recognized early on that the experience of carrying, birthing, and surrendering her birth daughter would likely shape her life. And so it has.

EMMA F. CONNOLLY lives and writes with her husband and 3 rescue dogs in Memphis, Tennessee and serves as a deacon in the Episcopal Church. She also leads writing workshops to empower urban women and girls to tell their stories.

KIMBERLEY HORDER CRAIG is a busy mother of four beautiful boys, ages 7, 5, 2 1/2, and 3 months old. She and her husband run a child care center with 24 employees and 165 children. Kimberley has a unique perspective on adoption. Adopted at birth, she also placed a son for adoption when she became pregnant at age 15. She has met her own birth mother and hopes to meet her son someday.

ROBIN L. FLANIGAN is a freelance writer. She lives with her husband and daughter in Rochester, New York, where she finds peace in practicing her personal mantra: *Know what you want. Work hard to get it. Accept what comes next.*

COLLEEN JUHL HARRYMAN is a writer. She lives in Minneapolis with her husband and daughter.

JOANNE LEEMING: Born in Cambridge, but now living near Liverpool, Joanne, 44, is the mother of Amy, 22 and David, 19. She is grandmother of Kieran, aged 5. Joanne works in a school office full time and fills her spare time seeing family and friends and studying for a degree in Humanities with the Open University.

TERESA MARTIN and her husband Tim have adopted multiple children through Child Protective Services. Teresa works as an RN in El Paso, Texas and Tim works as a Religious Education Director.

MOLLY McCAFFREY teaches at Western Kentucky University, works for Steel Toe Books, and documents her life as a non-dieter at *I Will Not Diet*. Nominated for a Pushcart Prize, an AWP Intro Journals Award, and Scribner's Best of the Fiction Workshops, she received her Ph.D. from the University of Cincinnati. Her work has appeared in numerous magazines and books, and she is currently editing an anthology of short fiction called *Commutability: Stories about the Journey from Here to There*, to be published in the fall of 2010. She lives in Bowling Green, Kentucky, with her husband, novelist David Jack Bell.

NATALIE McNABB graduated from the University of Washington with distinction in English. She lives and writes in Newcastle, Washington, USA. Recent and upcoming publications include fiction and poetry for *Scrivener's Pen Literary Journal, InterSECTIONS, Bricolage Literary and Arts Journal*, Fish Publishing, Ilura Press and W. W. Norton & Company.

JESSICA POWERS is the author of *The Confessional* (Knopf, 2007), a young adult novel exploring race, violence, and religion on the U.S.-Mexico Border. Her forthcoming young adult novel, *This Thing Called the Future* (Cinco Puntos Press, 2011), is a coming of age novel set in South Africa during the AIDS epidemic. She is the publisher of Catalyst Book Press and blogs at www.jlpowers.net.